D0920353

What Others Sa

"Years after Elaine served as Chairperson of FPSB, the organization overseeing CFP certification globally, people continue to refer to her as a great example of a financial planner with strong leadership skills, deep intelligence and a true dedication to the profession of financial planning. People are naturally drawn to Elaine for many of the skills that help her build lasting relationships with clients - her warmth, her candor, her big-picture thinking and her determination to always make principled decisions based on a strong sense of ethics. I've enjoyed working closely with Elaine in establishing financial planning as a global profession, one that always puts the needs of clients first. If my legs were longer, I would also have enjoyed joining Elaine on those 5 A.M. runs."

Noel Maye, CEO, Financial Planning Standards Board Ltd.

"Elaine Bedel is one of the true veterans of the Financial Planning profession. She is one of the smartest and most insightful people I know, and her long service in support of the CFP® credential, both in the U.S. and around the world, gives her an authentic global perspective very few other people can bring to their work for their clients."

S. Timothy Kochis, Chief Executive Officer & Principal, ASPIRIANT

"Financial guru Elaine Bedel helps thousands of Hoosiers - both novices and seasoned investors alike - become financially fit through her series of Money Sense columns in *Indianapolis Woman* magazine. Whether it's dispensing advice on how to emerge from a mountain of debt or navigate the complex stock market, Bedel motivates readers to ultimately change their lives with a sensible, easy-to-understand approach."

Mary B. Weiss, President / CEO, Publisher, Indianapolis Woman and St. Louis Woman Magazine

"Elaine has a unique ability to break down complex financial matters and then effectively communicate with any audience. That special talent, along with her commitment and passion for the profession, have earned her deserved recognition as one of the nation's most respected financial advisors."

Gerry A. Dick, Creator and Host, Inside INdiana Business with Gerry Dick

"Elaine is one of the true leaders in financial planning. Over the more than twenty years I've known her, she has worked tirelessly for the financial well being of her clients. She has contributed profoundly to the professional community on the local, national and international level. My colleagues and I have benefited from Elaine's rare mix of poise, brains, authenticity and energy."

Marilyn Capelli Dimitroff, CFP®, Capelli Financial Services, Inc. & 2008 Chairperson CFP Board of Standards

"Elaine Bedel has shown her desire to help people improve their financial lives in many ways—in her practice working with her clients, or sharing her knowledge and experience with professional financial planning organizations in the United States and abroad. Elaine also shows her unselfish desire to help all levels of the socio-economic structure in America through her leadership on the Board of Trustees of the Foundation for Financial Planning, a charitable organization helping Americans in need take control of their financial lives. Be it client, professional peer or the underserved, through *"Advice You Never Asked For, But Wished You Had"* Elaine is again helping people improve their financial lives."

James A. Peniston, Executive Director, Foundation for Financial Planning

"Elaine Bedel is one of the most clear thinkers in the financial planning profession. Her concern for the field is matched only by her care for her clients."

Ross Levin, CFP®, ACCREDITED INVESTORS, INC.

Advice You Never Asked For...

But wished you had!

To Cindy,
Thank you for your friendship over all the years. I look forward to continuing to share successes in the future.
Elaine

Advice You Never Asked For...

But wished you had!

Questions Answered About Financial Planning:

Estate Planning ~ Investing ~ Protecting Your Credit

Retirement ~ Health Care ~ Renting vs. Buying

Financing Higher Education ~ Much More

Elaine E. Bedel

CERTIFIED FINANCIAL PLANNER™

Copyright © 2009 by Elaine E. Bedel, CFP®

All rights reserved.

No part of this publication may be reproduced, stored in a retrieval system, or transmitted, in any form or by any means, electronic, mechanical, photocopying, recording or otherwise, without the prior written permission of the copyright owner.

This publication is designed to provide general information prepared by professionals in regard to subject matter covered. It is sold with the understanding that the authors are not engaged in rendering legal, accounting or other professional service. Although written by professionals, this publication should not be utilized as a substitute for professional service in specific situations. If legal advice or other expert assistance is required, the service of a professional should be sought.

Bedel Financial Consulting, Inc.

www.BedelFinancial.com

Printed in the United States of America

ISBN- 978-0-9819537-0-0

About the Author

Elaine Bedel, CFP®, has more than 30 years experience providing financial planning and investment management services for executives, professionals and entrepreneurs. She is president and founder of the Indianapolis-based wealth management firm, Bedel Financial Consulting, Inc., which achieved its twenty-year milestone in 2008. The firm works with clients to achieve financial security and accomplish their lifetime goals.

Elaine has earned the respect of peers around the globe while serving on the boards of numerous national and international financial organizations, such as the U.S. CFP Board of Standards and the international Financial Planning Standards Board. She currently serves on the board of the national Foundation for Financial Planning. Elaine has been recognized as one of the leaders in her profession by national financial magazines— *Bloomberg's Wealth Manager, Worth Robb Report, Worth Magazine, Financial Planning Magazine, Mutual Funds Magazine* and *Medical Economics*— most recently being named to Wealth Manager's 2008 "50 Distinguished Women in Wealth Management" list. She has been named to "Bloomberg's Top Wealth Managers" list every year since its inception in 2002.

An accomplished speaker, Elaine is often requested to speak at local, national and international organization events and conferences, and to provide her expertise to local and national television and radio shows as well as Internet magazines. Currently she is a weekly contributor to Inside Indiana Business e-newsletter, The *INside Edge,* and writes a monthly financial column for *Indianapolis Woman* magazine.

Elaine still finds time to serve her alma mater, Hanover College, by serving on the Board of Trustees, and to assist her community, serving on many local boards, including the Women's Fund of Central Indiana and Goodwill Industries Foundation. She has two grown sons and lives in Indianapolis with her husband Eric and their two dogs. She enjoys running, golf, hiking in the mountains and traveling around the world.

Table of Contents

Preface i

Chapter 1 - Making Informed Financial Decisions

Choosing a Financial Planner 1

Your Financial Game Plan 5

Financial Planning Advice for Career Starters 7

Overspending: Is it ever okay? 9

What to Keep and What to Toss 13

Chapter 2 - Protecting Your Credit

Credit Cards: Use them wisely! 17

Holiday Shopping: Don't let it ruin the New Year! 20

Credit Reports and Scores 22

Lock Down Your Credit Reports 25

Identity Theft: Avoid being easy prey! 27

Chapter 3 - Spending on Homes and Education

First-Time Homebuyers: Beware the extra costs! 31

Your Home: Renting versus buying 34

Mortgages: Choose the program that fits your needs 37

Time-Share Purchase Versus "Pay-as-You-Go" 40

Saving for Education 42

Financing Graduate School 46

Chapter 4 – The Art and Science of Investing

Asset Allocation: Get it right! 51

The ABCs of Mutual Fund Fees 54

Stock Market Investing Is Not for Sissies! 57

Beta = Measurement of Market Risk 61

When Interest Rates Go Up, Why Do Bond Values Go Down? 64

"Strong Dollar," "Weak Dollar:" What's it all mean? 66

Chapter 5 - Finances and the Workplace

Best Advice for Your 401(k) 69

401(k) for the Self-Employed 73

About Individual Retirement Accounts 76

Inappropriate Investments for Your IRA 81

What You Need to Know About Stock Options 84

Employer Stock in Your Qualified Plan: An alternative to rolling it over 88

Chapter 6 - Family Affairs

Women and Money 93

Teach Kids to $ave, $pend and $hare 96

Managing Family Finances During Uncertain Times 98

Life Insurance: How much do I really need? 102

Caring for Parents 105

Even Gift Cards Come With Instructions! 109

Chapter 7 – All About Health

Who Will Make Health Care Decisions When You Are Unable? 111

Using Pre-tax Dollars for Health Care 113

Medicare Coverage 116

Do I Need Long-Term Care Insurance? 118

The Indiana Long-Term Care Insurance Program and the Indiana Incentive 120

Chapter 8 – Retirement Considerations

Retirement: Is it an option for you now? 123

Spending Wisely During Retirement Years 125

Combine Your Retirement Accounts and Simplify Your Life 127

Making Sense of Minimum Distributions 130

Which Pension Benefit Should I Take? 132

Is My Pension Guaranteed? 134

Social Security Retirement Benefits 137

Chapter 9 – Paying Attention to the Details

Five Easy Steps for Gifting Stock to Charities 141

Strategies for Low Cost Basis Stock 144

Proving Tax Deductions Without Cancelled Checks 147

Micro-Business Owners and 1099 Forms 149

Chapter 10 - Till Death (or Divorce) Do Us Part

Letter of Instruction 151

Dealing with the Death of a Spouse or Partner 153

Divorce: Understanding your finances 156

Second Marriages: Planning, prenuptials and peace of mind 158

Chapter 11 - You Can't Take It with You

What Is Estate Planning? 161

Estate Planning and Simple Wills 163

Minimizing Estate Tax 165

Should You Give the House to the Kids? 167

Chapter 12 – Your Financial Toolbox

The Valentine Checklist: Show your loved ones you care 171

Year-End Tax-Planning Checklist 174

Preface

"Everyone Needs a Financial Plan."

There is no getting around it. Financial planning is everyone's personal responsibility—at least everyone who wants to ensure their future financial security. The process begins by answering a few questions: Can I afford a house? How much life insurance do I need? Is it necessary to have both a will and a trust? What is the best way to save for college? How much in assets do I need to retire?

Once you answer these, and other important questions, the appropriate actions to take will become more apparent. After that, the only requirement is for you to follow your action plan to ensure your family's needs can be met.

Everyone needs a financial plan, but not everyone needs a professional planner. Many individuals choose to make informed decisions by doing their own research. If this sounds like you, you are looking in the right place. This book was created to assist the "do-it-yourselfer" of any age, as well as others, who want simple explanations and answers to common questions. It is a place to begin your financial journey and an easy reference to obtain specific information along the way. It is not, however, meant to provide legal or accounting advice. Any questions about your unique situation need to be addressed by the appropriate advisor.

Advice you never asked for...but wish you had is for all you curious people who don't have time to read an entire book to find the answer to one question, but who do have time to read a succinct article that explains one targeted issue and provides you with enough guidance to reach a decision. Each chapter consists of several related, but self-contained articles. Simply browse the Table of Contents for the topic you want to pursue and go straight to that article.

The articles in this book were originally published in *The INside Edge*, the e-newsletter produced by Inside INdiana Business and Gerry Dick. In addition, several topics served as the basis for articles that have appeared in *Indianapolis Woman* magazine, published by Mary Weiss. My thanks to them both for allowing me to share articles on a regular basis with their readers. I am grateful for the editing talents of Shari Held and the formatting skills of Amy House who finally made this book a reality.

And a special thanks to Bedel Financial Consulting clients, my associates and friends for the questions and suggestions that became articles. This book is for you.

Chapter 1

Making Informed Financial Decisions

Choosing a Financial Planner

Financial planning is the key to achieving your goals. Choosing the right professional to work with is as important as choosing your child's pediatrician. You want someone you feel comfortable with, someone to whom you can ask questions and discuss issues. You also want to have confidence that the advice you receive is credible and on target for your needs.

Everyone needs a financial plan. Some people can do it themselves with assistance from online calculators, financial planning literature and investment research. Others choose to work with a financial planning professional. There are many reasons for someone to seek the services of a professional. Often a sudden change in a financial or life situation, such as an inheritance or serious illness, requires immediate attention. Others look for a financial planner because they do not have sufficient time or a keen interest in doing the necessary research to make their planning decisions on their own.

If you are among those looking for assistance, there are several factors to consider when choosing a planner: educational background and experience, how the planner will work with you and how he/she is paid for services rendered.

Education and experience. When interviewing the potential planner, understand his/her educational background and experience level. Most financial planners today began their careers in the investment, insurance, accounting or banking industry and received a large amount of their knowledge and experience on the job. Since financial planning is now offered as a degree program in many colleges and universities, in the future, a greater number of planners will have received a significant portion of their knowledge from the classroom. The planner's background may influence his/her area of specialty. You want a planner with the experience that matches your needs.

Planning process. Determine how the planner will work with you. Ask him/her to explain the steps that he/she will use to understand your situation provide the analysis and make the recommendations. Ask whether a written plan is provided and the type of follow-up that you should expect. You will also want to understand whether the planner will assist in implementing the recommendations. The planner may provide certain services in-house, such as investment, insurance or tax preparation, or he/she may work with other professionals to assure the action items are completed. You should expect your planner to work with your existing professional advisors when necessary to assure the recommendations are implemented on a coordinated basis and that all professional activities complement each other.

Compensation. There are three ways that planners are compensated: fees from clients, commissions paid by a third party or a combination of both. During your initial contact with the planner, either by phone or in person, you should seek specific information concerning the planner's compensation structure. If the planner indicates he/she does not charge to do a plan, you may want to determine how comprehensive the service is and whether it will meet your needs.

- Fee-only planners. A fee-only planner is paid by the client for the services provided. The fee may be based on an hourly rate or on a project basis reflecting the complexity of the issues to be addressed in the plan. Some planners may base their fees on a formula using a percent of investment assets or net worth as a means to determine the fee.

- Commission-only planners. Some planners are compensated for working with you through commissions paid by a third party. These are generally commissions earned for the initiation of investment transactions or insurance sales.
- Fee-and-commission planners. A fee-and-commission planner may also be referred to as a "fee-based" planner. Generally a fee is charged for the creation of the financial plan, and commissions are earned if the plan is implemented with products that the planner offers.

Professional Designations

There are several professional designations that require a candidate to have specific levels of education and experience to qualify. For example, the CERTIFIED FINANCIAL PLANNER™ certification requires competency in over 100 financial topics. The educational requirement must be met prior to the comprehensive ten-hour exam. In addition to passing the exam, the planner must have three years of experience working with clients prior to publicly using the CFP® certification mark. To maintain the certification, the planner must complete the required hours of continuing education and adhere to a code of ethics and practice standards.

In addition to the CFP® certification, other financial-planning designations include the Personal Financial Specialist (PFS) that is sponsored by the American Institute of Certified Public Accountants and the Chartered Financial Consultant (ChFC) provided through the American College.

Regulatory Issues

Every financial planner is required to be registered as an investment adviser unless he/she qualifies for an exemption. The registration is either with the Securities and Exchange Commission (SEC) or the Securities Commissioner of the state in which the planner practices. The planner is required to disclose to you information about his/her practice and all professional staff. This information can be provided either through a brochure that has been approved by the SEC or the "ADV Part II" form that the SEC provides.

The SEC or the state Securities Commissioner will audit each planning firm periodically. You can determine whether the planner has incurred any violations by contacting the appropriate office. If the planner is also a licensed insurance professional, you can contact the state Insurance Commissioner to ask about any irregularities or violations that may have occurred in the planner's past.

Finding a Financial Planner

There are several financial-planning membership organizations that will provide names of planners in your geographic area. Both the Financial Planning Association (www.FPAnet.org) and the National Association of Personal Financial Advisors (www.NAPFA.org) provide a referral service. The CFP Board of Standards (www.CFP.net) can also provide helpful information about the financial planning process as well as allow you to confirm the status of a CFP® certificant.

Choosing a financial planner is an important task. Secure the names of several planners either through referrals from friends or business associates who use a planner, or through your own research. Interview each candidate either over the phone or in person. Ask your questions and review the information each provides. As important as selecting a planner that matches your needs is selecting one that you are personally comfortable with. After all, you will be sharing your information with this person and putting your future financial well-being in his/her hands.

Your Financial Game Plan

You need to have your personal "game plan" to be financially successful. Take time at the beginning of each year or some other designated time, such as an anniversary or birthday, to create your own strategy and to develop an action list to accomplish your personal goals.

Here are nine financial "tips" that can help you along the way.

1. **Goals.** It is important to write down your goals and keep them in a place where you are likely to read them at least once a week. Your electronic or paper calendar may be a good place. Reading your goals periodically will help keep you focused throughout the year.
2. **Spending.** Maintain the lifestyle you can afford. Buy only what you need, not what you want. Do not create "lifestyle debt." If you purchase "stuff" to keep up with the neighbors you will be threatening your future financial security.
3. **Credit cards.** Never carry a balance. Be smart and use your credit card wisely. While it can be an effective and efficient financial tool, financially savvy people charge only the amount they can pay off each month.
4. **Gift cards.** Many gift cards begin to lose value six months after the date of purchase. Read the fine print and plan accordingly.
5. **Saving.** Make your saving automatic. Decide the amount you must save based on your saving budget, and deduct it from your paycheck before it goes into your checking account. If you are saving to finance a college education, have the appropriate amount automatically deposited to a 529 Plan. If you are saving for retirement, have the appropriate amount deposited directly into your 401(k), 403(b) or other retirement plan. For other investments, have the funds directed from your paycheck to a brokerage account.

6. **Check your progress.** Get organized. Establish a system of tracking that will allow you to easily review your saving and spending budget throughout the year. Consider software and/or on-line banking.

7. **Five-year rule for stock investing.** Never put money in the stock market that cannot stay invested for at least five years. Money needed within five years should be invested in cash, money market or other fixed-income investments with a maturity that matches your timing for needing the money. Remember to always be diversified. Invest in large, medium, small and international stocks with both a growth and value orientation.

8. **Income tax.** Take advantage of all pre-tax benefits. Maximize your 401(k) or 403(b) contributions. Participate in the medical reimbursement account as well as the dependent care plan, if appropriate. Document all tax-deductible items.

9. **Important Documents.** Keep important documents up-to-date.

    - **Property insurance.** Review your property insurance to assure all assets are appropriately protected from loss. This includes homeowners, renters, vehicle and umbrella liability policies.
    - **Personal insurance.** Review your life, disability, health and long-term care policies to assure the coverage remains appropriate.
    - **Estate plan.** If your family estate is over the amount that can pass outright to heirs free of federal estate tax, you need a will that allows the family to take full advantage of estate tax credits. A “simple” will that passes all assets to the surviving spouse and then to children is no longer appropriate.

It takes commitment and discipline to control your finances. Make your financial "game plan" for the year and implement it diligently. If you do, you will be on track to reap both personal and financial success.

Financial Planning Advice for Career Starters

The best time to develop good habits in money management is when you begin your first job. The two most important priorities at that time are participating in a savings program and avoiding "lifestyle debt." Developing good money management skills now will serve you well in the future.

Living Within Your Means

The biggest mistake young professionals often make is spending beyond their means. Yes, you need to establish a saving and spending budget. As boring as it sounds, being disciplined about saving first and then spending the remainder will reduce future headaches and help you accumulate significant wealth. Regardless of the amount, start the habit by saving a portion of each paycheck.

A spending budget includes obligations such as rent, utilities and car payments. In addition, you may have a school loan that requires monthly payments. List these as fixed monthly obligations. Next, think about the annual payments that you are required to make, such as auto insurance and license, renters insurance, etc. Divide each annual payment by twelve and add it your list of monthly expenses. Total that amount and plan to set that amount aside each month. Then determine your work-related expenses such as gas, parking and lunch. The remaining amount is what you have left to cover food, clothing, personal grooming, gifts, entertainment, vacations and other expenses.

At this point, you may find that your planned expenses are more than your take-home pay. If that happens to you, first review your spending budget to determine your alternatives. For example, can you ride the bus to work and eliminate the need for a vehicle and all related expenses? Or, if the bus is not conducive to your work schedule, can you reduce your transportation costs by carpooling? Have you considered finding a roommate to share rent and other related costs? Figure it out. It is very important that you stay within your budget.

Avoiding Lifestyle Debt

You will have to be prepared to make tough spending decisions. You cheat your future by not saving or by taking on debt to live beyond your means. Too many young adults develop a bad habit of using their credit cards and not paying off the full balance when due. Credit card debt is generally created to support a lifestyle that your paycheck cannot. Lifestyle debt on a credit card is very difficult to pay off. If you only pay the minimum balance on your credit card each month, it will take you almost 40 years to get your balance back to zero—and this assumes you do not add any new purchases. Lifestyle debt is a black hole that should be avoided.

Participating in a Savings Program

Why is saving so important? Because the earlier you start, the easier it will be to achieve your goals. If you have time on your side, even saving a small amount on a regular basis can make a big difference.

The best way to save is to make it automatic. Many employers have a retirement savings plan. This program will generally allow you to save a portion of each paycheck. The added benefit is the "employer matching contribution." The employer may match your contribution up to a specified amount. For example, a common formula is a match of 50 cents for every dollar you contribute, up to six percent of your pay. By contributing at least six percent, you receive another three percent.

Make it your goal to save at least the amount that will be matched by your employer. Then as your income increases, take the opportunity to increase your contribution beyond that amount. To demonstrate the impact of saving as early as possible, consider the following example:

> *At age 22, your first job pays you $30,000. You decide to save six percent of your salary in order to receive the full employer match. This means that during the first year, you will contribute $1,800 and the employer will match with another $900. For purposes of this example, assume that you never increase*

this amount. If your funds earn an average annual rate of return of eight percent, you would accumulate approximately $700,000 after forty years, or age 62. If you delay saving for five years, by age 62, you accumulate only $465,000. If you decide to spend all your income and not save during the first ten years, you accumulate only $300,000. Delaying your saving by ten years reduces your accumulated funds at age 62 by more than half. If you choose to spend and not save, you are cheating your future.

Overspending: Is it ever okay?

Is it ever okay to spend more than you earn? It is not uncommon to experience a time in your life when you cannot live within your means, but unbridled spending can have disastrous results. You must understand the consequences and plan for your recovery.

Whether overspending is "okay" depends largely on the reason for the excessive expenses and your ability to play catch-up in the future. Overspending can be categorized as either "emergency," "planned" or "lifestyle."

Emergency overspending. In today's economic and business environment, workers may find themselves unemployed due to downsizing, company mergers or business relocations. Personal illness or disability and family emergencies may likewise cause a loss of earnings. Under these circumstances, a family will find themselves spending more than they are earning for a period of time. In most of these situations, the intent is to become re-employed. Therefore, overspending as a temporary event cannot be avoided.

Planned overspending. Living beyond your income can also occur to meet a specific goal such as providing the desired educational experience for your children, celebrating a special event or assisting with necessary parental or other family member needs. If you have decided that accomplishing these goals is an important priority for you and your family, you need to include these expenses as part of your overall financial plan. It is important to consider how and when you can financially recover from these obligations. Thinking through the impact of achieving the goals will indicate the consequences. Barring no sudden receipt of wealth, you may sacrifice other lifestyle choices in the future and be required to work longer to accumulate sufficient funds to provide for your own retirement.

Lifestyle overspending. Overspending to enjoy a lifestyle that cannot be supported over the long run cannot be justified as "appropriate." The consequence is a continued increase in debt. At some point in time, you will be required to make significant sacrifices. In most cases, irresponsible spending will end in bankruptcy. The consequence of bankruptcy is future difficulty in securing loans for a home, vehicle or other personal use. If you are able to secure a loan, it is likely you will pay a higher interest rate than other borrowers. Even if you have the ability to recover from bankruptcy, the stress of financial issues can be devastating to a family and is often a contributing factor to divorce. If you find yourself in this situation, you need to seriously reassess your priorities, make major adjustments in your living expenses and begin to accumulate assets, not liabilities, for your future.

Funding Options for Emergency Overspending

If you are spending more than you are earning, you should review your personal financial situation to determine the most appropriate means of overcoming the shortfall. The following options should be considered. Your solution may be a combination of several options.

- **Reduce spending.** Your first reaction should be to review your spending budget and make changes wherever possible.

- **Reduce saving.** If your spouse is working and making regular contributions to a savings program, the amount can be reduced or eliminated while the family recovers from the temporary setback. You should re-institute this saving habit as soon as possible.
- **Spend emergency funds.** Having an emergency fund equal to three to six months of income is the appropriate manner to plan for the sudden change in your financial situation. If you have accumulated an emergency fund, this is your first source for replacing the lost income.
- **Utilize personal investment portfolio.** If the emergency overspending period extends beyond your reserve funds, the next source to access may be your personal investment portfolio. Because liquidating your investments may create income tax or penalties, you should evaluate this alternative against borrowing the funds to meet your needs.
- **Secure a home equity loan.** A good option for funding in an emergency situation is a home equity loan. This source for funding can be established in anticipation of the need with a financial institution. The advantage of this over other types of debit is the tax deductibility of the interest.
- **Careful use of credit cards.** Credit cards offer the quickest and easiest, but most expensive, means of meeting unforeseen expenses. Use this source only if you truly believe the excess spending will occur only for a short time.
- **Tap your life insurance cash value.** A universal or whole life policy that has a built-up cash value may provide a source for borrowing. The policy will require the payment of interest on the borrowed amount, but you are not required to repay the principal within a certain time period. If the insured person dies prior to repayment of the loan, the death benefit will be reduced by the outstanding loan amount.

- **Secure a personal loan.** You can secure a personal loan to meet your needs, but the interest will not be tax deductible. Unless you have significant assets to use as collateral, you may have a difficult time securing a personal loan if you are unemployed.

The cause for overspending can be unavoidable or planned. If you are prepared for the unexpected, you can recover from the temporary setback. Likewise, if you create a financial plan that includes the achievement of your priority goals, you will have a road map to follow that will allow you to get back on track after the planned overspending.

Be aware that chronic overspending to enjoy a lifestyle that your own financial resources cannot sustain will end in disaster. There is no remedy for lifestyle overspending.

What to Keep and What to Toss

We are often advised to "get rid of the clutter" and "simplify our lives." As your file drawer gets cramped, you may get the urge to "pull and dump." But before you do, review the guidelines regarding the length of time you should maintain your important records.

Income tax returns. Retain these permanently. After seven years, you can discard the supporting documentation, but keep the actual returns. The IRS has three years to raise routine questions about your tax returns and six years for under-reporting of income. The IRS has no time limitations in cases of fraud. Your tax returns document your life, e.g. place of employment, earnings, address, etc.

Bank accounts. Keep cancelled checks for one year, unless the payment is tax-related. Keep tax-related checks with your tax returns. Monthly statements can be disposed of after each year's tax return has been prepared. Withdrawal and transfer slips can be disposed of after the transactions appear correctly on your monthly statement. For tax purposes, deposit slips should be kept for seven years as evidence of the source of funds.

Credit card statements and receipts. Retain statements until that year's tax return is filed, unless they are needed for long-term tax records. Then keep them with your tax return. Retain receipts until they appear correctly on your statement. Once a purchase appears on your statement, your statement can serve as your record. Exceptions are receipts for items that you may want to return, that are under warranty or that are tax related. Retain tax-related receipts with your tax return.

Paycheck records. Maintain the final pay record for the year, which shows the accumulated totals. All others can be discarded. The final pay record should be used to verify the information on your W-2 form.

Investment records. For tax purposes, maintain "purchase" confirmations as evidence of cost for seven years after the investment is sold. The "sale" confirmations can be disposed of when the transaction is correctly reflected on your statement. Monthly statements should be maintained until the account is closed and the information is no longer needed for tax purposes. In some cases, a year-end statement can be kept in place of the monthly statements. This is only advisable if all purchase and sale transactions are individually identified on the year-end statement.

IRA records. Retain these for seven years after you close your IRA. You will need to retain records showing non-deductible contributions until the funds have been withdrawn and appropriately taxed. Form 8606 on your tax return should be a good substitute for illustrating non-deductible contributions.

Social Security reports. Maintain your current annual statement illustrating earning and projected benefits. Once you have verified that your earnings have been reported accurately, the previous year's statement can be destroyed.

Autos, boats and other vehicles. Keep all documents of ownership while you own the vehicle, e.g. title, warranties, registrations, etc. If the vehicle is sold, the transfer of title and license plate transfer records should be maintained. All other records can be disposed of unless there are legal claims pending.

Insurance policies. For home, auto and other vehicles, you can dispose of the policy when there is no possibility of a claim *and* the policy has been replaced or the property disposed of. For life insurance policies, dispose of terminated policies only when there is no cash value and when there is no chance of reinstatement (usually five years). For health insurance policies, dispose of only after they are totally expired or lapsed. Any paperwork related to claims should be maintained at least one year after payment or for seven years if tax related.

Residence records. Retain these for seven years for tax purposes after you sell or move.

- If you own your residence, you need to maintain purchase-related documents, mortgage and tax-assessment papers, receipts for improvements, etc.
- If you have inherited your residence, maintain the estate tax return showing the value.
- If you rent your residence, maintain a copy of your lease, cancelled checks and any correspondence or agreements with the landlord.

Personal information. Maintain the following certificates and papers permanently: birth/death certificates, marriage/divorce certificates, religious ceremonies, diplomas, adoption/naturalization papers, military discharge papers, court orders on personal issues, passports and Social Security cards. You may want to maintain a copy of these documents in your home file and the originals in a safe deposit box.

Wills and trusts. Dispose of obsolete original documents and any copies that have been made. Once you totally rewrite a will or trust, the obsolete documents should be destroyed. If you amend a document, the original document must be retained with the amendment. For any terminated or liquidated trusts, the documentation should be maintained for seven years for tax purposes.

Protect your identity and shred! Many of the documents that you may decide to purge from your files contain information that should remain confidential and secure. This includes account numbers, investment amounts and Social Security numbers. For this reason, it is advisable to shred these items instead of tossing them in your wastebasket. If you do not, you may be setting yourself up for identity theft.

Chapter 2

Protecting Your Credit

Credit Cards: Use them wisely!

A credit card can be an excellent financial tool or a stake through your financial heart! It all depends on how you handle it.

There are over one billion credit cards in use in the United States. In year 2001, according to Consumer Credit Counseling of Nebraska, credit card purchases exceeded $400 billion with an additional $50 billion of interest expense. The average family has five credit cards and an outstanding balance of over $8,000.

Great Financial Tool

A credit card can make your life easier. A credit card can eliminate your need to carry a lot of cash. You can purchase almost any product or service immediately and have additional time to gather the dollars. A credit card facilitates commerce by allowing you to purchase products or pay bills over the phone or the Internet. In short, it is difficult to live without one!

If you pay off the total balance due each month, you are managing the use of your credit card. Your credit card is then a "convenience" and not a method of living beyond your means.

Stake through Your Financial Heart

If you mismanage the use of your credit card by charging purchases you cannot afford, you are handicapping your financial future. It is easy to do. Everyone wants everything immediately. It takes discipline to manage your budget and save for the extras. But beware: not paying off the balance is the "stake to your financial heart." When the interest begins to accrue, it becomes harder and harder to catch up.

Many credit cards charge zero- to five percent for an "introductory" time period. Remember, there is no free lunch! You are not going to find a credit card company that will allow you to borrow money and not pay for the privilege. You can continue to roll balances from one "great deal" to another each month, but eventually the game will come to an end and you will need to "pay the piper."

Minimum Payments Mean Maximum Headaches Long-Term

Several years ago I heard a statement that made me shake my head. An individual commented to a friend, "I only pay the minimum due each month on my credit card. I'm not going to give them any more than I have to." That person was basing his payment strategy on emotion. That is not a wise financial strategy. Unfortunately, this person is not alone. Twenty-five percent of credit card holders pay only the minimum balance.

If you only pay the minimum due each month on your credit card, it will take you almost 40 years to pay off the balance! This is assuming you do not add any more purchases!

College Students and Credit Cards

During Freshmen Orientation, local financial institutions set up booths and encourage students to sign up for credit cards. At least five "approved" credit card applications appear unsolicited in the mail for a student each month. A college student can get a credit card by simply signing his/her name. No proof of income or any ability to make the financial commitment is required. Unless parents are paying the bills, this "convenience" tool can quickly become a problem that impacts the student long after graduation.

According to a study released in July 2002 by Nellie Mae, a provider of higher-education student loans, 83 percent of college students own credit cards. Approximately 54 percent of college freshmen use credit cards. That percentage increases to 92 percent by the sophomore year. The average credit card debt in year 2001 was $2,327 per student.

Unfortunately, almost 50 percent of college students with credit cards leave school with poor credit records due to the mismanagement of their credit cards. This will impact their ability to get car loans, rent apartments or transact any business where a credit report is crucial.

A debit card or a "prepaid" credit card can be used to allow students to have the convenience of a credit card without the opportunity to wreck their financial futures. The debit card will only allow them to spend the amount in their bank accounts. A "prepaid" credit card is similar to a phone card. You purchase it for a set amount and when it is spent, the card is no longer usable.

Tips for Using Your Credit Card

If you want the convenience of a credit card without the headaches of credit-card debt, follow these tips:

- Maintain a minimum number of cards, preferably one.
- Track your purchases during the month to prevent charging more than you can pay.
- Check your statement carefully to immediately detect any fraudulent use.
- Pay off your balance each month!

Holiday Shopping: Don't let it ruin the New Year!

When retailers believe consumers are going to increase holiday spending, retail company stocks rise. This may be good for your stock portfolio, but deadly for your finances in January. Remember to approach your holiday shopping in a responsible manner so that the "joy of giving" doesn't ruin your New Year finances.

For many people, the day after Thanksgiving signals the start of the holiday shopping season. Although this day is not the biggest shopping day, it is in the top four, according to shopping statistics. The biggest shopping day is the Saturday before Christmas. Unfortunately for some, procrastination often leads to overspending. It can be better for you and your budget to start early and be prepared.

Before You Go Shopping...

- **Make a list.** List the people you are buying for and the dollar amount you would like to spend. Once you total the dollars on the list, consider the impact this will have on your budget - can you afford it? If not, revise the list accordingly.
- **Research your gift idea.** First decide the amount you can spend and then decide what to buy. Next, do your research on pricing, instead of just going to the mall and making your purchases. The Internet is a useful price-comparison tool. According to the U.S. Department of Commerce, 36 percent of Americans use the Internet to search for products. There are many comparative shopping sites, referred to as "shopping bots", that will provide prices for specific products from a variety of vendors. BizRate, DealTime, MySimon and PriceScan are examples of shopping bots. Even if you plan to shop in a local store, check Internet prices first.
- **Decide where to purchase**. Purchasing online or from a local store may depend on several factors, such as the item, the price and the amount of time you have. Through your research, you

may find that the best price is available from a store ten states away or from an Internet-only venue. Remember to check the quality along with the price. There are certain products, e.g. books, movies and music that are perfect for purchasing over the Internet. You know what you are getting, so quality is not an issue. When purchasing digital equipment, such as a camera, it is best to purchase a name brand. Before you purchase online, determine whether you need to add shipping and handling charges. After adding in the extra costs, you may find a better deal from the local store. Be sure to consider the delivery time. If time is of the essence, you may find yourself fighting the crowd at the mall.

- **Use coupons to save bucks.** Once you decide on the gift, look for the coupons. The local newspaper is one source. The Internet is another. You can find coupons from manufacturers as well as retail stores online. Value-pak, ValuePage, HotCoupons and CouponPages are examples of sites that offer printable coupons.

Credit Cards Versus Cash

Using credit cards to make your purchases can be convenient. You can purchase almost any product or service immediately and have additional time to gather the dollars to pay for it. A credit card facilitates purchases over the phone or Internet. However, if you find it is too easy to overspend when you are using your credit card, consider taking only cash on your shopping trips. You will be more aware of your spending and more likely to stick to your budget.

Credit cards can allow you to postpone the payment into next month's budget. However, the reality of paying the bills in January can ruin your budget for months to come. For example, let us assume that you use a credit card for your shopping and that the credit card charges18 percent annual interest for unpaid balances. For every $1,000 that goes unpaid on a credit card for a month, another $15 is added to the cost of your giving. Three months of interest can cost you a dinner out!

Tip for Next Year

Establish a gift saving account in January. Determine the amount you would like to spend for gifts next December. Divide the amount by the number of paychecks you will receive in the next eleven months. Arrange for the calculated amount to be direct-deposited from each paycheck to the gift savings account. If you use this discipline, the funds will be available when needed and you will avoid the budget crunch in December and January.

Holiday gift giving can be fun and personally satisfying. Or it can be a time of great stress and anxiety. Decisions on gifts, budget concerns and time crunches can ruin your holiday spirit. To relieve the stress, get organized and do your research before you shop. This may save you dollars, time and stress!

Credit Reports and Scores

Before you make an application to rent an apartment, meet with a banker to request a loan or start the interviewing process for a job, you should check your credit history. Your credit report contains information that may influence the outcome.

Credit Reports

Your personal credit report includes information about your financial behavior and outstanding credit balances. It will provide specific credit account information such as the date an account was opened, the loan amount or credit limit, the current balance and monthly payment amount. It will also indicate whether you have missed payments or been consistently late.

The credit report will also contain "public record information." This category may include bankruptcy information, overdue child support and tax liens. Once this information is included on your credit report it can remain there for seven to fifteen years. Bankruptcy information can remain on your report for up to ten years, and data concerning tax liens for up to fifteen years.

The credit report will also indicate the number of times your credit information has been requested. A third-party request for a credit report is generally provided after you have given consent by signing a waiver included in your loan or job application. However, the Fair Credit Reporting Act does allow a financial institution to receive your credit information without your consent in some cases.

The report will include your name, current and past addresses, your employment status and names of past employers. You or a creditor can also add a temporary dispute statement when an account status is challenged.

You should check your credit report at least annually or before making an application for a loan or interviewing for a job. You want to be sure the information is error free and accurately represents your financial history. There are three agencies that provide credit reports. You can call or go to their Web sites to request a report.

- Equifax Information Services, 800-685-1111, www.equifax.com
- Experian (TRW), 888-397-3742, www.experian.com
- Trans Union, 800-888-4213, www.transunion.com

The cost of a credit report is usually $8 to $10. However, since December 2004, consumers can get a free copy of their credit reports once a year.

Credit Score

Based on your credit report, a financial institution will calculate your credit score. The credit score is also referred to as a risk score. The financial institution will use the score as a predictor of your ability to repay the loan. The score is generated by a statistical model that uses the credit report information along with other information obtained from your application, such as annual income and equity in your home.

Your credit score can be used as a determining factor for the approval of your request, as well as the interest rate that may be charged for the loan. Generally, the lower your credit score, the higher your borrowing rate.

Improving Your Credit Score

Negative information can remain on your account for seven years or longer. Therefore, it is important that you protect your credit rating by managing your finances appropriately and by reviewing your report on a regular basis for accuracy. Improve your credit scores by doing the following:

- Review your credit report annually and immediately correct any errors.
- Make your payments for credit cards, car loans, apartment rent or other financial obligations on time. If necessary, provide an explanation for any late or delinquent loan payments.
- Keep the number of inquiries to your credit report as low as possible by minimizing the number of credit card applications that you submit. Each time your credit report is requested by an entity or individual, it is noted on the report. Too many requests may give the impression that you are desperate to secure credit from many sources.
- Request that positive information be added to your credit report to indicate financial security.

A lender or potential employer is not going to rely solely on your credit report and credit score when making a decision, but it will be an influencing factor. The best advice is to be diligent in managing your current finances so you have a positive credit rating.

Lock Down Your Credit Reports

Identity theft continues to be a concern for all consumers. You should take action now to protect your credit information. Denying unauthorized access to your credit reports is one way to curtail the activities of identity thieves as well as the resulting financial damage that you can suffer.

Security Freeze

Indiana passed a law on September 1, 2007, that would allow any consumer in Indiana to place a "security freeze" on his or her credit report. A security freeze prevents a credit reporting agency from releasing your credit report information without your consent. Without access to your credit report, financial institutions will not approve a loan and credit card companies will not issue a credit card to someone posing as you. This can help to prevent the damage that can be created by an identity thief who has other personal identifying information, such as your Social Security number.

If you choose to request a security freeze, be aware that it may slow down or delay certain personal or business transactions due to the time required to give legitimate access to your reports. Credit reports are always checked when you apply for a loan or credit card, rent an apartment, purchase a cellular phone, sign up for utilities, or even apply for employment. So if you have placed a security freeze, you will need to plan ahead to have the freeze removed when credit report access is needed to transact your business.

A security freeze will generally not apply to creditors who have an existing relationship with you requiring periodic review of your credit report.

How to Place and Remove a Security Freeze

To place a security freeze, you will need to mail your request to each of the three credit reporting agencies (Equifax, Experian and Trans Union). After January 1, 2009, each of the three agencies is required to provide a secure electronic mail connection. In your request, you will need to provide the following information:

- Full name, address, Social Security number and date of birth.
- All mailing addresses used during the last five-year period, if you have moved during that time.
- Proof of your current address such as a current utility bill or property tax bill.
- A photocopy of a government-issued identification card such as a driver's license, state ID card or military papers.

For your convenience, the sample letters to each of the three credit reporting agencies provided by the Consumers Union are available on our Web site (www.BedelFinancial.com) in Word format.

You should expect the credit-reporting agency to initiate the freeze five business days after receiving your letter. Within ten business days of placing the freeze, each of the agencies will send to you a confirmation letter. In the letter, you will receive a unique PIN (personal identification number) or password that you will be required to use to temporarily or permanently remove the freeze.

You will need to request the freeze be removed to allow you to conduct any business requiring a credit report. Before 2009, the credit reporting agency has three business days to process your request to lift the freeze. However, after January 1, 2009, the agencies will be required to remove the freeze within fifteen minutes.

You can contact each of the credit reporting agencies by phone, fax or Internet to remove the freeze either temporarily or permanently. You must provide the following information: sufficient identification to verify your identity, your PIN or password and the time period that you want your credit report to be available to all requestors or the specific name of a creditor(s) who should have access.

For Indiana residents, there is no fee charged by the credit reporting agencies to place, temporarily remove or permanently remove the freeze.

Identity Theft: Avoid being easy prey!

Identity theft may not be the worst thing that can happen, but it ranks pretty high! According to the Federal Trade Commission, identity theft is increasing at an alarming rate, with an estimated 9.9 million victims from year 2002 alone. Identity theft can take both time and money to resolve. What can you do to avoid this frustration? You must protect your personal information and remain alert to fraudulent activities.

Identity Theft Defined

Someone pretends to be you. He/she opens up credit cards, siphons money from your bank account, receives a personal loan or negotiates contracts with your good name and credit record. These are only a few of the problems created if you are a victim of identity theft.

Identity theft can involve any of the following fraudulent activities:

- Using an existing credit card account by simply knowing the number.
- Opening a new credit card, utility or cell phone account.
- Writing checks or using a debit card on your existing bank account.
- Getting money by securing a personal loan or line of credit in your name.
- Purchasing a car with a loan in your name.
- Renting an apartment in your name and skipping out a few months later.
- Getting a job under your name and Social Security number.

First Line of Defense

Identity thieves can get your personal information in a variety of ways. Your information is available legally though the court system, county tax records, licensing agencies and even the U.S. Postal

Service. We also provide our personal information voluntarily through Internet activities, emails and surveys that we complete in return for a free gift or discount. Other information is obtained by stealing your wallet or purse, your mail or even your trash.

Here are a few suggestions for keeping your personal information private:

- **Protect your Social Security Number.** Institutions that report tax information such as your employer and financial institutions need your SSN. Those who need to check your credit record such as lenders, landlords and credit card companies also require it. The motor vehicle department, tax department and welfare department are also legitimate requesters. But it is generally not required by other businesses that may ask for it. Do not provide it unless it is absolutely necessary.
- **Wipe out the hard drive.** Before donating or throwing away your computer, be sure to clean all information from the hard drive. Even if it is not up-to-date, it may provide the information necessary to steal your identity.
- **Check transactions.** Before you automatically pay your credit card bill or file your checking or saving account statements, review the transactions carefully to be sure you can identify and verify each one. Thieves may start with a few small charges to your credit card or withdrawals from your checking account to see if you notice. If you do not, larger ones will come in the following months.
- **Buy a shredder.** Shred, instead of trashing, any kind of account statements, pre-approved credit card offers, paid bills, credit card receipts, etc. Any piece of paper that has your personal information and any account number is a valuable commodity to an identity thief.
- **Say "no" to information sharing.** Request that your personal information not be shared with other companies when you receive the annual privacy statements. Taking the time to "opt-out" may be time well spent.

- **Protect your mail.** Putting up the flag on your mailbox is a sure sign to the thief that valuable information is inside. It is better to take your bill payments to the post office to be mailed rather than having them picked up by the mail carrier. Also have a neighbor remove your mail from the box while you are out-of-town. Account statements and unpaid bills may be used as proof of identity by some unsuspecting vendors.
- **Protect your passwords.** Forego using obvious passwords like your mother's maiden name or numbers that are part of your address. Keep the passwords in a secure place or do not write them down at all. When using a PIN or password, be aware of "shoulder surfers" who may be trying to observe as you punch the keys.

What Do I Do If It Happens To Me?

First, contact one of the three credit reporting agencies (Equifax, Experian or TransUnion) to put a "fraud alert" on your report. That agency will notify the other two. If the report is checked, the potential creditor should refuse to grant the loan or open the new credit account.

Immediately close any existing or new accounts that have experienced fraudulent activity. In addition to financial institutions, this may also include phone companies, utilities and other service providers. If a checking account is involved, close the account and destroy the remaining checks.

Contact the local police and file a report. They may not be able to assist in resolving your issues, but the report may be needed to validate your claims with creditors and vendors.

Contact the Federal Trade Commission and file a complaint. The phone number is 1-877-IDTHEFT (438-4338). For online information, go to: www.consumer.gov/idtheft.

Identity theft is a serious problem. Unfortunately, the majority of the responsibility to prevent and, if necessary, resolve the situation will fall to you. Begin now to reduce your chances of being a victim by protecting your personal information.

Chapter 3

Spending on Homes and Education

First-Time Homebuyers: Beware the extra costs!

It is easy to calculate the mortgage payment when buying a home, but what about immediate repairs, replacement of appliances and the increased maintenance costs? All homebuyers, but especially first-time homebuyers, should consider their *total* financial obligation before committing to the home of their dreams.

The real estate agent and the mortgage lender play a major role in setting your expectations by calculating the mortgage debt that you can qualify for based on your income and other liabilities. Add to this the property tax and the homeowner insurance premium. Many times the decision to purchase is based only on the family's ability to pay the monthly mortgage amount. This can be a mistake.

Now that you have found the home of your dreams, slow down and look at the costs for immediate repairs, appliance replacement and annual maintenance *before* signing on the dotted line.

Home Inspection

Prior to purchasing a home, participate in the home inspection. The cost of an inspection is generally $150 to $500. It will be worth the time and money to be sure that you have a complete understanding of the condition of the house. You will receive an inspection report, but you should also take good notes. The information that you gather will give you an idea of the required maintenance costs involved in purchasing the house, or may even cause you to reconsider whether to purchase the property at all.

The inspection will include items that relate to the integrity of the structure, such as the foundation, framing and electrical system. If a major issue that was previously unknown is uncovered in these areas, you may reconsider whether to purchase the home or, at least, reduce the offering price to compensate for the defects.

The inspection will also include a thorough analysis of the items that require periodic maintenance, such as the roof, siding, plumbing, heating systems, storm drainage, etc. The report will indicate the age and remaining life of the items, as well as reveal any items that need immediate repair. The costs for the immediate repair items should be considered in the price negotiations with the seller. More importantly, this area of the inspection can provide insight as to your future financial obligations. This information will help you determine whether the house is really affordable.

In addition to the structural and periodic maintenance items, the inspection will also point out the condition of interior surfaces such as the flooring, counter tops and interior wall coverings and paint. Since these items are cosmetic in nature, you can plan the expenditures over time.

How Much Will It Really Cost?

From the inspection report and your notes, you should have a good idea of what you will need to replace, and a timetable for making replacements. You can create your own schedule for the next one to five years and begin setting aside funds in the "House Maintenance" account each year to meet the costs. The table below may provide some guidance.

Item	Life in Years	Cost	Monthly Set-Aside
Roof	10	$2,524	$21.00
HVAC	13	$5,461	$35.00
Refrigerator	6	$820	$11.39
Oven	6	$984	$13.66
Washer	8	$591	$6.16
Dryer	8	$535	$5.57
Exterior paint	6	$4,100	$56.94
Windows	15	$15,000	$83.33
Doors	15	$6,876	$38.20
Driveway	9	$4,802	$44.46
Heater	8	$1,013	$10.56

Source: Askthebuilder.com

Budget for Maintenance

The senior research fellow at Harvard University's Joint Center for Housing Studies, Kermit Baker, says that you should plan on spending one percent of the value of your house (excluding the value of the land) on maintenance each year. For example, if you pay $250,000 and the lot is worth $50,000, you should reserve $2,000 per year (one percent of $200,000). Using this rule of thumb, you should increase the amount each year to reflect inflation. Accumulating any unspent funds in your "House Maintenance" account each year will prevent a sudden financial burden when the maintenance or replacement is due. This reserve fund will also make it possible to do the repairs as needed instead of delaying them. All the research shows that it is important to take care of the problem immediately and not delay. Delaying almost always increases the ultimate cost.

Put It All Together

The mortgage, with property tax and homeowners insurance included, and the annual maintenance are a large portion of the cost of owning a home. But remember to consider the monthly utilities and the immediate purchases that you will need to make, such as a lawnmower, snow shovel/blower and furniture!

Do your research and plan your budget. Make sure the home you are purchasing is both physically comfortable and financially affordable.

Your Home: Renting versus buying

The decision to rent or purchase your place of residence should be considered from several aspects: your financial commitment, your need to be flexible for relocation and your preference for lifestyle. While home ownership is the American dream, there are times when renting may be the more comfortable option.

People just beginning their careers almost always rent an apartment in the city where they land their first job. This is the most practical option for someone who is moving into an unfamiliar location and has no money for a down payment. Likewise, if the first job does not meet expectations, a renter has more flexibility to consider other options.

Getting married and starting a family tend to trigger the first thoughts for purchasing a residence. Double incomes may make the financial transaction easier, and by that time the couple may have a stronger commitment to their careers and location.

But these two life events, i.e. first job and getting married, are not the only times when the question of renting versus buying will surface. Both the tangible and intangible benefits need to be considered.

Financial Aspects of Renting vs. Buying

There are many items to consider when putting together a total financial picture that compares renting versus buying.

- Both renters and buyers make monthly payments, but there is a difference. As a buyer, the mortgage payment remains steady. There may be predictable changes based on future adjustments to the borrowing rate throughout the life of the mortgage. Unfortunately, the rent payment may increase with each new lease agreement.
- Renters do not need to make a down payment equal to 10- to 20 percent of the purchase price of the home. Homeowners can, however, deduct interest paid on the mortgage on Schedule A. The cost to rent is not deductible on your federal tax return, though some states may provide a renter's deduction or credit.
- Homeowners are required to pay general upkeep, maintenance and utility costs. Renters have the potential to direct these dollars to their retirement savings vehicles and other investments.
- Renters pay less for insurance since they are protecting only the contents of their respective apartments. Each homeowner must insure the home itself, as well as the contents.
- Renters do not pay property tax; homeowners do. However, property tax is a deductible item on Schedule A.
- If the budget gets too tight, it is easier for a renter to downsize than it is for a homeowner.

A Residence as an Investment

While not guaranteed, the value of a residence may increase over time. This may allow some or all of the expenses of homeownership to pay off in the long run.

- Homeowners experience market value risk; renters do not. As with any real estate, there is the potential for the residence value to increase or decrease. As an example, a homeowner will have little control over the impact that a new commercial, retail or residential development may have on the existing neighborhood.

- A homeowner is continuously increasing his net worth, since a portion of each mortgage payment increases the equity in the home. All of a renter's payment goes to increase the landlord's net worth.
- Real estate is not liquid. Unlike a stock or mutual fund that can be sold at any time for the market value, it may take months to find a buyer when a house goes on the market. Therefore, a renter will find it easier to relocate for employment, convenience or family reasons than will a homeowner.

Lifestyle Benefits of Renting

Besides financial benefits, consider the differences in amenities and lifestyle.

- Amenities available in rental communities such as pools, tennis courts and exercise facilities, that naturally lead to social networking, may not be affordable if you purchase a home.
- Renters will be required to spend less time on the general upkeep of their residence, such as yard and garden work, and therefore have more leisure time.
- A renter does not have the worry and does not bear the cost of damage to a residence and the resulting clean-up in the aftermath of a natural disaster.

From a pure dollars-and-cents point of view, owning a home is generally a good investment over the long-term. However, if a no-hassle lifestyle with the ability to be flexible is appealing to you, renting may be a better option. Financial issues should always be considered, but during some periods of your life the intangibles may be more important.

Mortgages:
Choose the program that fits your needs

Remember when the 30-year fixed was your only mortgage option? Today you can have a fixed- or variable-rate mortgage with amortization over 15, 20, 30 or even 40 years, or you can even pay interest-only. Here is a look at the different mortgage programs to help you determine which one best suits your needs.

Fixed Mortgages

A 30-year fixed-rate mortgage remains the most popular type of home loan, especially for first-time homebuyers. The desire to have the mortgage paid off by retirement induces some homebuyers in their mid-40s or older to consider the 15-year fixed-rate mortgage. The 15-year mortgage will generally have a lower interest rate than the 30-year mortgage. The rate difference and the shorter amortization period results in a significantly lower amount of interest paid to the lender.

> ***For example:***
> *A $100,000 loan amortized over 30 years with an interest rate of 5.875 percent will have a monthly payment of $592.The monthly payment for a 15-year loan with an interest rate of 5.25 percent will be $804. The total interest paid to the lender for the $100,000 borrowed is $113,000 over the 30-year loan period and $45,000 for the 15-year loan.*

Using the example above, if your cash flow allows, you can make an additional payment of $212 per month on the 30-year mortgage and pay off the debt in half the time. That would reduce the total interest paid by $68,000, enough to buy several cars! If the loan is for $200,000, you can double the numbers and the savings.

Variable-Rate Mortgages

A variable-rate mortgage will generally have a lower interest rate than a fixed mortgage. The lender is willing to give you this lesser rate knowing that the opportunity exists to change the rate periodically to reflect the current market. In a market with rising interest rates this type of mortgage financing may present a risk to the homeowner. If the interest rate increases, the monthly mortgage payment will increase as well.

Variable-rate mortgages come in a variety of packages. For example, a "3/1 ARM" (adjustable rate mortgage) is a 30-year mortgage program that allows the initial interest rate to be fixed for the first three years. At the end of year three, and every year thereafter, the interest rate is subject to change. The new rate is based on an identified current market rate and is limited to increasing or decreasing within the range defined in the mortgage contract. Other variations of this type of mortgage include the "5/1 ARM" or "7/1 ARM." These mortgages work the same as the "3/1 ARM," but the fixed-rate period is either five or seven years.

The benefit of a variable-rate mortgage is the ability to have a lower initial payment. The risk is the potential for the interest rate to increase and, consequently, increase your monthly payment. Your option is always to refinance to a fixed rate, but the fixed rate then is likely to be higher than the fixed-rate option at the time of the original mortgage. You will also incur closing costs to refinance. Obviously, if the interest rates decrease over the time period, your monthly payment decreases, and you win the bet!

Before you consider the variable-rate mortgage option, calculate the current payment and the payment at the end of the first fixed period, e.g. three, five or seven years, assuming the interest rate increases to the maximum allowed in the contract. Then decide if the higher payment is still within your budget. Always consider the "worst case scenario."

The variable-rate mortgage is an ideal vehicle if you plan to stay in your home for only a limited time. For example, if you know that your employer is transferring you in two years, the "3/1 ARM" may be perfect. Likewise, if you know a larger home will be needed in six years, a "7/1 ARM" may be appropriate. It is important to match the mortgage program to your expected plans for staying in your home.

Interest-Only Mortgages

There are mortgage programs available that allow you to pay only the interest on the loan for a period of years. For example, a 5/25 interest-only mortgage is a thirty-year mortgage that will allow the borrower to pay interest-only for the first five years. Beginning in year six, the principal and interest are amortized over the remaining time period of 25 years, with the interest rate changing every six months. There are also multiple versions of the interest-only mortgages. Each varies the interest-only period and the amortization period, i.e. 3/27, 7/23, 10/20.

The benefit is the ability to purchase a home with limited cash flow. One disadvantage is the delay in paying the principal and, therefore, building equity in your home. A second disadvantage is the shorter principal amortization period and the interest-rate adjustments every six months.

This type of loan may be very beneficial for a homebuyer who is still making a mortgage payment on a previous home. Cash outlay can be minimized while waiting for the first home to sell. Once the house is sold, the interest-only mortgage can be refinanced to a more appropriate vehicle.

Factors to Consider

To determine the appropriate mortgage, you must consider your family's monthly cash flow, how long you plan to stay in the house and timing issues with purchasing the new and selling the old home. In addition, there may be other personal factors influencing your decision.

Likewise, there are more mortgage options available than those discussed above. Take the time to understand the options and how each works with your personal situation. It is always advisable to first consult with a knowledgeable mortgage lender or your financial advisor.

Time-Share Purchase Versus "Pay-as-You-Go"

As you contemplate a change of climate, should you consider the purchase of a time-share? If it suits your style for vacationing, it may be a perfect fit, but be aware that there are pros and cons to this investment.

What Does It Cost?

The cost to purchase a time-share unit can be as low as $7,000 or as high as $20,000 plus. This sum will buy you a place to stay for one week in a specific location. To maintain your investment, you will be required to pay an annual fee that can range from $300 to over $1,000.

When considering this type of an investment, remember that the initial payment and the annual fee do not pay for your vacation each year. You still need to pay for the cost of transportation, food, entertainment and other expenses that allow you and your family to have an enjoyable time. Yes, these expenses would be necessary even if you did not own the time-share. However, it is easy to forget these costs when you are in the midst of negotiating the purchase.

To determine if you can afford this investment, consider what you normally spend for lodging during vacation and whether you go on vacation each year. For families that do not vacation each year, it is likely that "pay-as-you-go" would be the better option. You may be successful in renting your time-share in the years you do not vacation, but you should not count on that. Likewise, if you are generally successful in searching out bargain prices for hotels, i.e. off-season pricing or Internet bookings, the time-share investment may prove more costly.

There is a secondary market for selling your time-share unit, but you can only expect to receive approximately half its original value. You also need to be sure you are dealing with a reputable company and that you do not lose your investment due to its poor management or financial condition.

Consider Your Vacation Style

If you prefer space, the apartment-style lodging offered by time-share units may be to your liking. Amenities such as kitchenettes and washers and dryers are available with some hotel rooms, but at a higher cost.

Unless you want to vacation at your time-share unit every year, you will need to plan ahead to swap for another location. The ease of swapping will depend to a large extent on the appeal of your unit and the popularity of its location. The more upscale you prefer to be, the more costly your initial investment.

If you like the convenience of full-service restaurants, spas, tennis courts, golf courses and other extras, you will need to research before you purchase or swap time-share units. These resort-type amenities may be available with a time-share unit, but never take it for granted or you may be disappointed.

Evaluating the cost to purchase a time-share unit is only a part of the decision to buy. For those who prefer variety, flexibility and spontaneity, the "pay-as-you-go" vacation may be more appropriate.

Saving for Education

Saving for college is important. With the increased cost of education, more parents and grandparents are seeking methods to efficiently and effectively accumulate funds for education. Understanding the two most popular programs—the Coverdell Education Savings Accounts and the 529 Savings Plans—and the differences in their benefits, can help you meet your goal.

Knowing your options can increase your ability to meet your child's needs, as well as your long-term strategy. There are multiple differences between the Coverdell Education Savings Account and the 529 Savings Plans, but there are two that are particularly important as you develop family savings strategies. The first is the control of the funds, i.e. child or parent. The second is the ability to use the funds for all levels of education versus just post-secondary. Keeping these factors in mind can allow you to develop a financial strategy to accomplish multiple goals for multiple generations.

Increased Education Costs

The cost of college is increasing each year at a rate higher than inflation. With the reduced funding for public colleges and universities by the state government, a larger portion of the education costs falls to the student. Private institutions are also increasing their price tags as programming and facilities are improved and increased to keep up with the demands of students and the competition from peer institutions.

According to the College Board, a national nonprofit membership association, average costs for the 2007-2008 school year increased to $23,712 for private four-year institutions (a 6.3% increase over last year) and to $6,185 for public four-year institutions (a 6.6% increase over last year).

Those figures alone are an incentive for parents to start saving. Here is a look at the similarities and differences in the two most popular programs for saving for education.

Coverdell Education Savings Account (formerly Education IRA)

The Taxpayer Relief Act of 1997 created The Education IRA, which was revised by the Economic Growth & Tax Relief Reconciliation Act of 2001, and then renamed the Coverdell Education Savings Account. This savings program is exclusively for the purpose of paying educational expenses. Each year taxpayers can make a $2,000 maximum, nondeductible contribution to a Coverdell account, for each beneficiary under 18 years of age. The income earned each year is deferred and remains untaxed if it is used for education expenses.

The Coverdell account can be used for education expenses for kindergarten through high school, as well as college expenses. Qualified expenses include tuition, fees, books, tutoring, room, board, supplies and equipment. It also includes computer equipment or technology and Internet access used at home by the student and family, as long as the account beneficiary is in school.

A contributor can establish multiple Coverdell accounts (each with one named beneficiary), but if a parent and a grandparent establish an account for the same beneficiary, the total contribution by both parties cannot exceed $2,000 per year. Unfortunately, the $2,000 annual contribution limit is phased out for tax filers with a high modified adjusted gross income. This phase-out income range changes for each tax year, which may restrict many potential contributors from using this vehicle. The $2,000 contribution is also subject to the gift-tax rules, which allow an individual to gift up to a specific amount ($12,000 in 2008) to as many individuals as desired without a gift tax.

Distributions from a Coverdell Education Savings Account are excludable from gross income to the extent that the distribution does not exceed qualified education expenses (net of any tax-free scholarships received). Any balance remaining in the Coverdell account at the time a beneficiary reaches age 30 must be distributed to the beneficiary. The earnings portion of such a distribution will be included in the gross income of the beneficiary and subject to an additional 10 percent penalty tax because the distribution was not for educational purposes. However, it is also possible to roll over any remaining amounts to the account of another qualifying beneficiary, such as a sibling who is under the age of 30.

It is important to note that the beneficiary has control of the account and is considered the owner, even though a parent or guardian is serving as the custodian. The custodian of the account must administer the account for the benefit of the child. All withdrawals are paid to the beneficiary and not to the person who established the account.

Since the Coverdell Education Savings Account is considered an asset of the student and not the parent, it can be a disadvantage when applying for federal financial aid. Federal financial-aid programs assume 35 percent of the value of the account is available for the child's education costs, versus a lesser 5.6 percent of the assets owned by the parents. Each college establishes its own rules for inclusion of child and parent assets when determining financial aid, and may differ from the federal program.

529 Savings Plans

The 529 Savings Plans were created in the mid-90s by the federal government under Section 529 of the Internal Revenue Code. This legislation enables individual state governments to create college savings plans with special benefits. You can contribute to a 529 Plan in the same year that you contribute to the Coverdell Education Savings Account.

A 529 Plan is similar to the Coverdell account concerning non-deductible contributions with the tax-deferred accumulation of earnings and the tax-free distribution of earnings used for qualified education expenses. However, there are several differences.

You can contribute as much as you would like each year to a 529 Plan (as long as the amount does not exceed gift-tax provisions) versus the $2,000 limit per beneficiary in the Coverdell accounts.

Each 529 Plan sets its own lifetime limit for contributions to any one account, but it is generally over $100,000. A special provision allows a contributor to "jump start" a 529 Plan by contributing up to five years of gifts in one year. If you contribute five times the annual gift exclusion amount in one year, you cannot make an additional gift to the child under the annual exclusion during the remainder of the gifting year or the next four calendar years.

There are no adjusted gross income restrictions limiting the amount a person can contribute to the 529 Plan. Therefore, everyone is eligible to contribute.

The funds from 529 Plans can only be used to pay for post-secondary education costs. This would include any public or private college or university, as well as trade and vocational schools. Unlike the Coverdell account, 529 Plan funds cannot be used for elementary and secondary education.

There are no residency requirements for participation in a 529 Plan, so you can participate in the 529 Plan of any state. The funds can be used for higher education anywhere, including outside of your state of residence.

The owner of the account, which is generally the parent, has control of the account for purposes of distributions, withdrawals and changing the beneficiary. This provides several additional benefits over the Coverdell account. If the beneficiary has completed college and no longer needs the funds, the owner can change the beneficiary to another sibling, another qualifying family member or to himself/herself. There is no requirement that the funds be used by age 30 or that an individual be under the age of 30 years when named as the beneficiary.

The owner of the account also has the ability to withdraw the funds. Since the funds are distributed for purposes other than education, ordinary income tax and a 10-percent penalty are imposed on only the earnings portion of the non-education distribution. This flexibility allows you to use the funds not needed for your children's education for your own retirement.

At this time, 529 Plans may have a lesser impact on the application for federal financial aid than the Coverdell account, because the plans are not considered an asset of the student. However, this may change in the future. Individual educational institutions have their own unique formulas for determining aid, which may include both the 529 Plan and the Coverdell account balances.

Financing Graduate School

When borrowing rates are low, it is a good strategy to include the federally sponsored Stafford loans as part of your financing package.

Stafford Loans

The federal government facilitates Stafford loans to assure that all students who are qualified to attend an educational institution have the financial resources to do so. There are two types of Stafford loans: subsidized and unsubsidized. With a subsidized loan, the federal government pays the interest while the student is in school. With an unsubsidized loan, the student can pay the interest from the time the loan is initiated or let the interest accrue and be added to the loan balance during the time he/she is in school. For either type of loan, the student must begin to make a regular loan payment, including interest and principal, six months after school is completed. The graduate-school funding package may include both types of Stafford loans, along with grants and/or loans directly from the educational institution.

The interest rate on Stafford loans is established on July 1st of each year. This means that each year that the student applies for the loan, the rate may be different.

Student as Independent

Parents apply for federal loans when the student is an undergraduate. However, it is appropriate for the student to apply as an independent person for the graduate school loans. Under this scenario, only the financial resources of the student are included in the calculations that determine the amount of outside funding necessary to provide for all education expenses. Likewise, this formula does not assume a financial contribution on the part of the parents. The government does not require information from the parents if the student is applying as an independent person for the Stafford loans. However, the graduate school's financial-aid office may require parent information for any grants or loans provided directly by the educational institution.

Steps for Applying For Graduate School Loans

Here is what the process of applying for Stafford loans entails.

1. First, the student completes a Free Application for Federal Student Aid (FAFSA) on-line. This is key to the process. It should be done as early as possible after January 1. The student's prior year tax return and asset information will be needed to complete the form.

2. On the FAFSA form, the student will indicate the graduate schools that are being considered or, after the first year, the educational institution that he/she is attending.

3. The FAFSA is processed and approved by the government and then forwarded to the school(s) listed.

4. The financial-aid department of each school uses the information on the FAFSA along with its funding formula to determine the amount and type of aid for which the student qualifies. This may include the government loans as well as the educational institution's own loan and/or grant program.

5. The school provides the student with a financial-aid package that includes sufficient funds for tuition, books, fees and living expenses. The school also provides a list of financial institutions through which the loans can be secured.
6. The student works directly with a loan provider to complete the loan process.
7. The financial institution provides the funds directly to the school. The school transfers funds to be used for living expenses to the student.

Loan Consolidation

After the student completes his/her education, the loans received over multiple years may be eligible to be consolidated into one loan. The interest rate on the single consolidated loan is based on the actual individual loan rates as well as the current rate. Depending on the future changes in the borrowing rate, consolidation may or may not provide a benefit to the graduate. Therefore, it's important to do the appropriate analysis before you take advantage of this convenience.

The Stafford loans may be forgiven in the event of death of the borrower. The loan document should be reviewed carefully to determine whether this provision is included.

Parental Assistance

Since the Stafford loans are considered the responsibility of the student borrower, parents who want to provide assistance can use the annual gift tax exclusion to provide funds to their son or daughter to make the payments. There is also no penalty for early pay-off of the loans. The annual gifting limit is increased every few years due to inflation.

Graduate school is an expensive endeavor. Often both the student and parents are involved in determining the appropriate financing for this level of education. With low borrowing rates and the interest-free or interest-deferred provisions of the Stafford loans, using this funding vehicle as part of the financial package may be a good use of the overall family resources.

Chapter 4

The Art and Science of Investing

Asset Allocation: Get it right!

Asset allocation is the most important aspect of your investment strategy. Your asset allocation dictates the amount of dollars invested in cash, stock, bonds, real estate or other types of investment vehicles. This is not a "one-size-fits-all" scenario. Your personal situation determines your asset allocation.

Asset Allocation Rules

When it comes to asset allocation, there are two basic rules to follow:

> ***Rule #1:*** *Do not invest in the stock market unless you anticipate leaving the funds invested for at least five years, preferably longer.*

The stock market will go up and down. This is a "fact," not a hypothesis. The history of the market shows us that money invested for at least a five-year period will likely reflect a higher value at the end of the period relative to the beginning. For a ten-year period, the probability of a gain is even greater. There are no guarantees, but investors who have the ability to keep their funds invested over a long period of time have been rewarded for their patience.

> ***Rule #2:*** *Funds that you need within a five-year period should be invested in the fixed-income arena.*

If funds from your investment portfolio are needed to pay next year's college tuition or replace an auto in three years, those dollars should be invested in vehicles that are expected to maintain their value. These dollars should not be subject to the risk of the stock market. Money market funds and certificates of deposit are the most stable investments. Corporate bonds and government bonds such as U.S. Treasury bills will remain fairly constant, but may fluctuate in value when interest rates or economic conditions change.

Determine Your Appropriate Asset Allocation

The appropriate asset allocation will protect you in a down-market and assist you in an up-market. The asset allocation used in your portfolio must be based on your particular situation, not that of a co-worker or relative, and must reflect your anticipated use of the funds. Here are two scenarios of how different people at different stages in life may allocate funds to fit their lifestyles.

- **Married with two children.** If you are age 35 and married with two children, ages 8 and 10, you need to save for college education, your retirement and perhaps an addition to the house. Your 401(k) or IRA funds can be invested in the stock market, since it is likely that you will not need these funds for at least fifteen years or more. The college funds can be invested in the stock market until the children reach high school. At that point, you will want to consider changing your allocation and investing those funds in a fixed-income vehicle. The money you are saving for the house addition next year must definitely be in fixed-income assets only. There is nothing more disappointing than to postpone a project because the stock market went down!
- **Retired married couple.** If you and your spouse are age 65, your portfolio will likely be very different from the 35-year-old couple in the former scenario. If you plan to withdraw $30,000 per year from your investment portfolio to supplement your pension and Social Security, you should have at least $150,000 (five years of distribution needs) invested in fixed income. Depending on the

size of your portfolio and your overall financial situation, you may want a greater amount in fixed income to provide more stability in your portfolio.

Change Your Asset Allocation with Your Situation

As you move through the different stages of your life, your asset allocation needs to be revised to reflect your needs. Today's asset allocation should be based on your need for funds over the next five to ten years. As your future needs change, your asset allocation needs to be adjusted. Changing status from a single person with no family responsibilities to a married person with children requires a change in your asset allocation, just as making a decision to retire in five years versus ten years does.

Do not get caught thinking you should invest your funds in the same manner as your neighbor. To successfully meet your financial goals, your asset allocation must reflect your unique needs. Think it through yourself or work with your financial planner or investment advisor to assure that this most important aspect of your investment portfolio is appropriate for you.

The ABCs of Mutual Fund Fees

Mutual funds are sound investment vehicles. They offer diversification and professional management. As an astute investor, you need to understand the choices you have concerning the different mutual fund fee structures before you purchase.

What Is A "Load?"

The term "load" refers to a sales charge. The load is calculated as a percentage of the amount that you invest and may be used to pay commissions to the person or institution handling your transaction. A mutual fund company establishes its own sales charge for each of its mutual funds. The legal limit is 8.5%, but many mutual funds charge less.

No-Load Versus Load Funds

You can invest in a "no-load" mutual fund without paying a sales charge. You do this by simply purchasing a no-load mutual fund directly from the mutual fund company. Since a sales person is not needed, 100 percent of the dollars involved in the transaction are reflected in the value of your mutual fund investment. For example, if you purchase $1,000 of XYZ no-load mutual fund, your resulting beginning investment value will be $1,000. Likewise, when you sell units of a no-load fund, you do not pay a sales charge.

You can choose to purchase a no-load mutual fund through a discount broker instead of establishing an account directly with the mutual fund company. In this case, you may be required to pay a small buy/sell transaction fee of $20 to $30 to the discount brokerage firm for the convenience of holding your mutual fund in a brokerage account. The benefit of using a brokerage account is the ability to hold mutual funds from multiple fund families in the same account, along with individual stocks, bonds, certificates of deposit, money market funds, etc.

A load mutual fund is purchased through a mutual fund sales person. A sales person can be employed directly by the mutual fund company, serve as an account executive with a brokerage firm or be someone who has passed the necessary exam to become licensed to sell mutual funds, such as an insurance professional. In each case, the sales person provides assistance in selecting and purchasing the load mutual fund. This assistance can be very valuable, and paying for such advice via the load that is charged can be very appropriate.

The ABCs of Load Fund Share Classes

A load mutual fund may offer several different methods for payment of the sales charge. The best option for you will likely depend on your overall investment strategy and the flexibility you want within your portfolio.

- **Class A shares.** If you purchase a Class A share, you will pay a "front-end" load. A front-end load is the most common method used by mutual funds. The maximum front-end load is 8.25%. Most front-end loads range from 3.5% to 6 percent. The front-end load reduces the amount that is actually invested on your behalf in the mutual fund.

  As an example:
  If you purchase $1,000 of a mutual fund with a front-end load of 5 percent, you will have a resulting investment value of $950.

  Investors who invest a large amount, or who commit to investing a specific amount over a period of time, will generally receive a "break-point" discount, which is a reduction of the front-end load. As an investor, you must be aware of this opportunity and plan wisely. For investors who achieve the investment break point by committing to invest a specific amount over time, it is important to follow up with the sales professional to ensure that you receive the appropriate reimbursement of the front-end load. After investigating the situation in 2003, the Security & Exchange Commission (SEC) and the National Association of Security

Dealers (NASD), the two regulatory agencies involved with mutual funds, found that 20 percent of the investors who should have received the break-point discount did not. If you believe that you fall into this category, you should contact the individual broker or brokerage firm that assisted in purchasing your Class A shares.

- **Class B shares.** With a Class B share of a mutual fund, you will not pay a front-end load at the time of purchase. Instead, you will pay a "back-end" load (also referred to as a "deferred contingency load" or a "contingent deferred sales charge") at the time of sale. The back-end load is charged if you sell your shares within a specified period of time after purchase. The required holding period to avoid the back-end load is usually four to seven years. Therefore, if you plan to hold the fund longer than the required time period, this share class may be appropriate for you. With this share class, you may lose some flexibility for the movement of funds within your portfolio.

  Many fund companies are eliminating the Class B shares. There has been some concern expressed by the SEC and NASD that there may be a built-in financial incentive for a broker to encourage investors to purchase Class B shares over Class A shares. Since there is no break point for large investments in Class B shares, as there is with Class A shares, some large investors may pay more to purchase the Class B versus Class A shares of the same mutual fund.

- **Class C shares.** A Class C share of a mutual fund will charge its investors an annual sales charge or a "level" load. This class of shares is generally less common than Class A or B shares.

The classes of shares available are fully disclosed in the mutual fund's prospectus. It is common for each share class to have a different internal administrative expense rate. When making your selection of share class you should also consider this difference. The percentages, holding periods and other pertinent information will all be provided in the prospectus. It is important that you review this information and consider your personal investment strategy prior to making your choice.

Mutual funds are excellent vehicles for investing in the securities markets. To create the portfolio that meets your investment strategy, you need to be knowledgeable of the different costs involved in purchasing the mutual fund units. Take the time to research your options and, if necessary, seek appropriate advice.

Stock Market Investing Is Not for Sissies!

Think of the stock market as a roller coaster ride. For example, we experienced down markets in 2000, 2001 and 2002 and saw 2003 usher in a rising market that stayed fairly steady over several years. If history has taught us anything, it is that nothing remains the same.

What Are Signs That A Bull Market Will Continue?

Because there are so many factors impacting the performance of the stock market, no one can answer this question with complete certainty. Positive signs in our economy would suggest that a bull market trend can continue. However, as we experienced in 2001, the market can be influenced by non-economic factors that are out of everyone's control.

What Can We Expect In A Prolonged Bull Market?

History suggests that we may not experience the same levels of returns in the second year of the bull market as we did in the first. Based on the analysis by Ned Davis Research, the second year of a bull market has an average return of 6.4%.

Have a Plan for Investing

While there is really no way to predict what will happen with the stock market, there are some "lessons learned" that provide a basis for sensible stock market investing. Having an appropriate investment plan can help you weather a down market and take advantage of a rising market.

If you invest inappropriately, you run the risk of getting hurt. For example, individuals who inappropriately invest money in the stock market that is needed for spending in the short-term will be required to sell in the down market. This results in a *permanent* loss of value.

> ***Lesson Learned:***
> *Write down your long- and short-term investment goals. Only funds that are can be invested for five or more years should be invested in the stock market. Keep funds needed within the immediate five-year period in the less volatile fixed-income investments, such as money market, certificates of deposit, bonds and U. S. Treasury bills.*

Stay the Course

During down years, investor concerns increase. As they see their funds diminish, some investors opt to sell for fear of losing more value. Those who do that may experience seller's remorse when the market rises.

> ***Lesson Learned:***
> *Long-term funds need to stay invested through the ups and downs of the market. If you do not need the money, leave it invested. History tells us to be patient and tolerant. A study of the market returns over all rolling five-year periods since the 1920s indicates a positive return in the vast majority of cases. This means that investing in year one and holding through year five will generally yield a positive return.*

Diversify Your Holdings

Investors who held only technology stocks during the late 1990s experienced a market value loss of as much as 80 percent during the following three years. During the same period, investors with a diversified portfolio experienced a loss, but more in the range of 25 percent to 30 percent.

> ***Lesson Learned:***
> *"Don't put all your eggs in one basket." It is really that simple. Invest in all sectors of the market. Diversify by size of company (large, medium and small), industry, geographic location (domestic and international) and investing style (value and growth). Consider no-load mutual funds that provide diversification among companies in each of the categories.*

When Should You Reinvest?

The dilemma for most investors who accumulate cash during a declining market cycle is how and when to return to the market. Historically, each down cycle has been short - with positive returns within a few days. However, when the market is down for longer periods, investors become leery. We all know the market can go down for a sustained period of time. That experience is really quite healthy. It reinforces the long-term nature of stock market investing. Consider this tactic for reinvesting.

- **Average into the market.** Invest funds over a three- to six-month period. For example, if you have $100,000 to invest, consider investing $15,000 at the same time in each of the next six months. This disciplined strategy will get you back into the market and allow you to avoid making all your purchases at the peak. Be smart. Accelerate your buying for that month if the market does take a dip, but make your purchases each month regardless of the direction of the market. Even if the market trends down for two months, continue to invest. Remember two things: buying low is always preferred and you are investing money for the long-term.

The caution that most investors feel when considering the stock market provides a healthy approach to investing. Remember that the stock market tends to reward those that invest for the long-term. To take advantage of this and be a smart investor, invest your cash over time in a diversified portfolio. Of course, you will need to monitor your portfolio and make any necessary changes. If you use mutual funds, you should review your fund's performance periodically against its peer group. Make a change if you feel your fund is lagging the performance of the category. Following this strategy should give you a smoother, more confident ride on the investing roller coaster!

Beta = Measurement of Market Risk

When discussing the performance of an investment, the financial news often quotes the "beta" of a stock or mutual fund. The higher the beta, the greater the market risk. Understanding the implications of the "beta factor" will help you assess your comfort level with the risk of your investment portfolio.

How Is The Beta Determined?

The term "beta" is used to indicate the risk of a specific security or investment portfolio relative to the overall market. The return of the market is measured by an index, such as the S&P 500, which is assumed to be the benchmark. The historical returns of a specific security are compared to the market returns. By analyzing multiple points in time, a statistical value is derived that relates the stock's return to that of the market. The beta provides an indication of how the stock price responds to market forces. This is also known as the stock's market risk.

The beta for individual stocks will generally fall within the range of .5 to 2.0. Since the overall market is considered to have a beta of 1.0, a stock with a beta greater than 1.0 will have a more exaggerated response to a market change, i.e. the stock will either increase or decrease more than the market average. Therefore, the higher the beta, the greater the volatility or movement of the stock price relative to the market. This price movement is one measure of the stock's risk.
A stock with a beta less than 1.0 will never be expected to gain or lose as much as the overall market. The lower the beta, the lower the expected volatility or risk. See the following example:

If the market return = 10%	**If the market return = -6%**
Stock with 2.0 beta returns 20%	Stock with 2.0 beta returns -12%
Stock with 1.5 beta returns 15%	Stock with 1.5 beta returns -9%
Stock with .5 beta returns 5%	Stock with .5 beta returns -3%

The vast majority of stocks will have a positive beta. If the beta is negative, the security moves in the opposite direction of the market. If the general market goes up, this security will decline. If the general market goes down, this security increases in value.

Since the calculation of the beta is based on the stock's past performance relative to the general market, there is no guarantee that the stock will continue to react to market forces in the future in the same way it did in the past. Changes in the company, whether intentional or unintentional, could affect its performance relative to that of the general market. Therefore, be aware that the beta of a particular stock can change and that it is not a guaranteed predictor of future performance.

What Does This Mean To The Investor?

In a rising market, it is to your advantage to own high-beta stocks. In a declining market, you would be better served to own low-beta stocks. Unfortunately, not many investors can successfully predict the market. Therefore, it is important for an investor to understand his/her particular risk tolerance and invest accordingly.

An aggressive investor is one who can tolerate dramatic moves in the value of his/her portfolio both financially and emotionally. This type of investor will tend to choose high-beta stocks for his/her portfolio. The aggressive investor is willing to assume the additional risk, realizing that the portfolio has the potential of earning a higher return than the market.

A conservative or risk-averse investor prefers to protect his/her portfolio in the event of a down market even if it means missing the "home run" in a bull market. The conservative investor will be more comfortable with low-beta stocks.

Measuring the Market Risk of Your Portfolio

The beta value is usually included in the analysis of individual stocks and mutual funds provided by independent research firms. To determine the beta of your portfolio of stocks or mutual funds, you must use a weighted average.

Here is an example of how this works with a $200,000 portfolio:

Dollar Value and Beta	Weighted Average
Mutual Fund A valued at $100,000 has a beta of 2.0	50% of portfolio X 2.0 = 1.0
Mutual Fund B valued at $50,000 has a beta of 1.5	25% of portfolio X 1.5 = .375
Stock C valued at $50,000 has a beta of .5	25% of portfolio X .5 = .125
Total Portfolio of $200,000 has a beta of 1.5	1.0 + .375 + .125 = 1.5

This portfolio's beta would indicate that the portfolio tends to respond to market forces 1.5 times greater than the overall market. Therefore, if the market increases in value by 10 percent, this portfolio may be expected to increase by 15 percent. Likewise, a market decline of 12 percent would tend to show this portfolio with a negative 18-percent return.

The beta of your portfolio is an important indicator of market risk. However, it is only one factor to be considered when developing your personal asset allocation and diversified portfolio. You should always consider your personal goals and your investing time horizon, along with other risk factors, when developing your investment strategy.

When Interest Rates Go Up, Why Do Bond Values Go Down?

When interest rates increase, you earn more on fixed-income investments. So why do bond values go down? It is the difference between being a seller or a buyer. Are you confused yet?

What Is A Bond?

When you purchase a bond, you are making a loan for a set period of years to the entity issuing the bond. That entity can be a company or institution, a municipality or the federal government.

The initial loan amount is referred to as the "par" value of the bond. The number of years is referred to as the "maturity" period for the bond. When the bond matures, the entity pays back the initial or "par" value of the bond. During the years until maturity, the owner of the bond receives interest based on the initial interest rate of the bond, also referred to as the "coupon" rate. Remember that when you purchase a bond, you are making a loan to the issuer of the bond. The issuer promises to pay the money back at the end of the loan period and pay you interest annually.

A bond can be purchased and sold through the bond market. This means that if you own a bond, but do not want to hold it to maturity, you can sell the bond to another person. The new owner will receive the interest payments for the remaining period until the bond matures. At maturity, the issuer of the bond will also pay the initial bond value back to the new owner.

Impact of Interest Rates on Bond Values

As interest rates increase, the value of existing bonds will decrease. This is a result of newly issued bonds paying a higher interest rate than existing bonds. If the buyer can purchase a new bond with a seven-percent coupon rate, why would he purchase an existing bond with only a five-percent coupon rate? The only way the new buyer would purchase the existing five-percent bond is if the bond could be purchased for some amount less than its initial or "par" value.

Inverse Relationship

Just remember: Interest rates increase and existing bond values decrease; interest rates decrease and existing bond values increase.

If you consider this inverse relationship from the point of view of a buyer or a seller of existing bonds versus newly issued bonds, the concept becomes clear.

> ***Simple example:***
> *We will assume you own a $10,000 corporate bond that pays a five-percent coupon or interest rate. This bond pays you interest of $500 per year. When the bond matures, the company will return the $10,000 to you.*
>
> *We will further assume that interest rates have increased since you purchased your bond and newly issued bonds are now paying seven-percent coupon rates. So for a $10,000 investment in a new bond, the owner can receive $700 per year in interest payments.*
>
> *If you want to sell your $10,000 bond paying five percent, you will receive only $7,143. This value is based on the new owner receiving interest of $500, which is seven percent of $7,143. Therefore, your existing bond is reduced in value to the level at which it pays the current interest rate of seven percent. Simply put, your bond is trading at a discount.*
>
> *The opposite happens as interest rates decrease. If your bond pays five percent and newly issued bonds pay only three percent, the value of your bond increases. A new buyer would be willing to pay more for the existing bond paying five percent than a new bond paying only three percent. In this case, your $10,000 bond is valued at $16,667. This is the amount at which $500 yields a three-percent return. Your bond is trading at a premium.*

This is a "simple example" because we did not take into consideration the years until maturity of the existing bond versus the new bond. That calculation is more complicated, but the concept is the same.

What to Do When Rates Change

As an investor, you invest in bonds because your asset allocation requires this asset class to meet your personal investment objectives. Bonds are generally considered less risky than stocks and are used to provide both stability and liquidity in your portfolio. Therefore, when interest rates change, this is not a signal to either purchase all bonds or sell all bonds. However, you can be a smart bond investor. If interest rates are expected to increase, you may want to own bonds with a shorter maturity. The closer a bond is to maturing, the less impact increasing interest rates will have on its value. Therefore, in a rising interest rate environment, you may want to sell longer maturity bonds and purchase shorter maturity bonds. In a declining interest rate environment, the opposite strategy would be appropriate.

"Strong Dollar," "Weak Dollar:" What's it All Mean?

Periodically the U.S. dollar declines in value against other world currencies. This weakening of the dollar can be both positive and negative. It is important to understand the impact of the change in currency value as we make decisions as investors and consumers.

Strong Versus Weak

When the dollar is referred to as "weak," it means that its value has declined relative to another currency, such as the Euro. For example, let us assume the U.S. dollar-Euro exchange rate is $1.20/Euro. This means that if you were in Paris and wanted to purchase an item priced at 10 Euros, you would pay $12.00. If the exchange rate moves to $1.30/Euro, you would be paying $13.00 for the same item. Because you must pay more U.S. dollars for the same item, the dollar has "weakened" against the Euro. Conversely, if the exchange rate moves to a more favorable $1.10/Euro, the dollar has "strengthened" against the Euro, and the item would cost only $11.00.

What Causes The Dollar To Fluctuate?

The simple answer is supply and demand. Just as the price of a stock changes based on the supply and demand of the shares, the value of the dollar fluctuates based on the supply of and demand for American currency.

One of the primary factors affecting the value of the dollar is the U.S. interest rate. Historically, foreign investors have been eager to buy U.S. Treasuries because they are considered a "safe" investment. To purchase U.S. Treasuries, foreign investors need to exchange their currency for U.S. dollars, thus increasing demand for the U.S. dollar and causing it to appreciate or strengthen against other world currencies. When the interest rate earned on U.S. Treasuries declines, the investment is less attractive to foreign investors and their money goes elsewhere, causing the dollar to weaken.

Consumer Spending

From the previously cited Paris example, you can immediately see the impact of traveling abroad when the dollar is weak. Not only will products cost more in the other country, but the hotel, meals and other services will be relatively more expensive as well. The opposite happens when the dollar strengthens. With a strong dollar, vacationing and doing business abroad becomes more affordable.

Since many of the goods that we purchase every day are made in other countries and imported to the U.S., a weak dollar causes the price of these items to increase. As consumers, the higher prices increase our personal cost of living.

Impact on Investing

There are benefits to a weakening dollar, however. For U.S. companies that sell their products overseas, a weak dollar makes their products less expensive compared to those of foreign producers. Likewise, it makes foreign goods imported to the U.S. more expensive compared to domestically produced goods. This increases demand here and abroad. More demand for their goods means more profits for the companies. This all translates to positive investment results for stockholders.

Investing in international stock companies can also have a positive impact from the dollar decline, but in a different way. The exchange rate can provide appreciation in a stock price and larger dividends to U.S. investors. For example, let us assume that the exchange rate with the Japanese yen is $1/125 yen and you buy one share of a Japanese stock trading for 1250 yen for $10. If the stock value stays the same (1250 yen) and the dollar weakens against the yen to $1/100 yen, then the dollar value of the stock would increase to $12.50. Without any change in the value of the Japanese stock, your value increased from $10 to $12.50, or 25 percent. The impact on a dividend payout would be the same.

In summary, the advantages and disadvantages of the fluctuating value of the dollar are complex. While a weak dollar presents some unique opportunities, it is important to note that this cycle does not last forever. Eventually the dollar will strengthen and the benefits will come to an end. Since no one can predict when these cycles will occur, as investors, it is important to maintain a diversified portfolio that includes both domestic and international investments.

Chapter 5

Finances and the Workplace

Best Advice for Your 401(k)

A 401(k) or similar plan is your best retirement savings vehicle. A 401(k) offers pre-tax contributions, tax-deferred earnings and "free money" (in the form of matched or other contributions from your employer) just for participating. If your employer offers a 401(k), you cannot afford to miss out on one of the best opportunities to save for your retirement.

What Is A 401(k)?

A 401(k) is an employer-sponsored retirement plan. It represents one of the best ways you can save for your future. If you work for a non-profit corporation, the 403(b) provides the same benefits as a 401(k).

The plan will generally offer a variety of investment options, such as bond and stock mutual funds, money market funds, guaranteed income funds and company stock. You can mix and match the options based on your overall investment plan.

There are three major benefits of participating in your employer's 401(k) program:

1. **Pre-tax contributions.** As an eligible employee, you can elect to have a portion of your pay directed to the 401(k) on a pre-tax basis. The amount you contribute throughout the year is a direct

reduction to your taxable income. If you are in the 35-percent marginal tax bracket, for every $1,000 you contribute, you will reduce your income tax by $350. If you are in the lower 15-percent marginal tax bracket, you still save $150 in taxes for every $1,000 contributed. Your contributions are not taxed until withdrawn.

The maximum amount you can contribute is determined by the tax code. If you are over age 50, you are eligible to contribute an additional "catch up" amount each year. Therefore, in year 2006, you can contribute a maximum of $15,000 to your 401(k) if you are under age 50. If you are 50 years or older, the maximum is increased to $20,000.

2. **Tax-deferred earnings.** The funds contributed to your 401(k) are invested per your instructions. Since the interest, dividends and investment growth occur inside the retirement account, your entire investment return is not taxed until withdrawn at retirement. All the earnings continue to be reinvested in your 401(k) account.

3. **Employer matching contributions.** In the majority of 401(k) plans, the employer will match a portion of your contributions. A common matching formula is 50 cents for each dollar you contribute, up to a maximum of six percent of your salary. This means that if you contribute at least six percent of your pay, your employer will contribute an additional three percent of your pay. This is free money that you forfeit if you do not participate. The employer match amount is invested per your instruction in the 401(k) plan and, like the contributions and earnings, is not taxed until withdrawn.

What Can A 30-Year-Old Expect At Retirement?

Here are several scenarios that exemplify how the savings can grow. For each one, let us assume that Jim is 30 years old and makes $60,000 per year. Jim's employer will match 50 cents for each dollar Jim contributes, up to six percent of his salary.

- Let us assume that Jim contributes six percent of his salary, or $3,600 per year. The company will contribute an additional $1,800 as its matching amount. Let us also assume that Jim is fairly aggressive with his investment selection and expects to earn an average of 10 percent per year until retirement at age 60. If we assume the same contribution and investment each year, by age 60 Jim will accumulate **over $1,000,000** in his 401(k).
- If we assume the same as above, with the exception that Jim contributes $13,000 each year through age 60, he will accumulate **almost $2,800,000**.
- Jim expects his salary to increase over the next 30 years, which means the matching by his employer will also increase. If Jim contributes the maximum allowed as it increases over time, his 401(k) has the potential to be much larger than $2,800,000.
- In addition to the accumulation in the 401(k), Jim has reduced his annual Federal and State income tax payment due to his contributions.

What If I Do Not Stay With My Employer?

If you go to work for another employer, you have two options. You can roll your 401(k) to your new employer's 401(k) or similar plan, if allowed by your new employer. The benefit of moving the funds to the new employer 401(k) is the opportunity to borrow funds from your 401(k). If the plan allows borrowing, this option can provide a safety net if you need money in the future. You must pay the loan back via payroll deductions. If you fail to pay the loan amount back into your plan, you will be required to pay tax and possibility a penalty.

Your second option is to roll the funds from your 401(k) to a Rollover IRA. Through the IRA, you have the ability to choose from the universe of eligible investment options. However, you cannot borrow from your IRA.

By rolling to the IRA or to the new employer 401(k) plan, your dollars continue to be tax-deferred. The transfer is done without payment of tax or penalties. Unfortunately, according to a survey by Hewitt Associates, 42 percent of employees taking 401(k) distributions in 2002 cashed out of their plan when changing jobs. Not only did these employees lose the ability to have the funds continue tax-deferred, they had to pay income tax on the total amount as well as penalties if they were under age 59 ½ years of age.

Automatic Deposit Makes Saving Easy

Since the percent that you elect to have directed to your 401(k) is never deposited into your checking account, there are no checks for you to write or transfers that you need to initiate. It is easy. And for most people, once they get used to not having it in their paycheck, the funds are not missed.

If you think you do not have the funds to put into your 401(k), review your spending budget and decide what amount you can start to save. If it is truly impossible to eke out a bit of savings, wait until your next pay increase. If you get a three percent raise, immediately start to contribute three percent to your 401(k). With each future raise, increase your 401(k) contribution.

401(k) for the Self-Employed

If you are a self-employed individual, the most effective retirement plan for you may be the solo 401(k). You can save more for your future retirement and receive a larger income tax deduction today.

Thanks to changes incorporated in the 2001 Tax Relief Act, the 401(k) retirement plan became a viable option for sole proprietors and small business owners. The solo 401(k) may allow you to save more of your income each year for retirement than is possible through other traditional plans, such as the Simplified Employer Plan (SEP), Keogh and profit-sharing plan.

This plan works for small business owners or sole proprietors with no employees other than a spouse. If you currently employ or plan to hire employees that work more than 1,000 hours per year, you will be required to establish a 401(k) or other retirement plan that includes those employees.

Contribution Amounts

The maximum contribution amounts may change each year. For example purposes, we are using the limits for years 2005 and 2006.
The maximum amount that could have been contributed to a solo 401(k) in year 2006 was the lesser of 100 percent of your compensation, up to $15,000; or 25 percent of your compensation, up to $44,000. (There was a $5,000 catch-up for those 50 years and older). The allowable contribution consisted of two parts:

1. One hundred percent of your compensation or self-employed income up to the amount indicated below:
   - Tax Year 2005: $14,000 ($18,000 if 50 or older)
   - Tax Year 2006: $15,000 ($20,000 if 50 or older)
2. Twenty-five percent of total compensation paid from the incorporated business or of self-employed net income.

For example:
If you were age 45 and received $100,000 compensation in 2005 from your small business, you could have contributed $39,000 ($14,000 plus 25 percent of $100,000) to your solo 401(k). This is significantly larger than the traditional small business profit-sharing contribution of $25,000. If your compensation was $112,000 or larger, you could have made the maximum solo 401(k) contribution of $44,000 ($49,000 if you were 50 years or older).

If your business was just getting started and your compensation was $14,000 or less, you could have contributed the entire amount to a solo 401(k). The solo 401(k) is an opportunity to shelter your entire income from taxation. This strategy may be possible if this is a "side business" and the family has sufficient cash flow from another source.

Advantages of a Solo 401(k)

Consider the advantages the solo 401(k) has to offer:

- **Higher contribution amounts**. You will generally be eligible to contribute a larger amount than allowed for other existing retirement plan options.
- **Ability to roll over funds from other plans**. You can roll over funds from former employer 401(k) plans, IRAs, SEPs, Keogh plans or Section 457(b) plans. This allows you to consolidate your retirement funds into one account.
- **Borrowing privileges**. You can receive a loan from the solo 401(k). The maximum loan amount is 50 percent of your balance, or $50,000, whichever is less. This is a distinct advantage over the traditional IRA account where loans are not allowed. If you need the flexibility to access funds currently held in an IRA, rolling the funds to a solo 401(k) will provide that access.

- **Investment flexibility**. You can establish a self-directed brokerage account as the custodian of the funds, giving you maximum investment flexibility.
- **No tax return**. As long as the total value of the solo 401(k) is under $100,000, you are not required to file annual plan reports.
- **Extended contribution date**. The contribution amount indicated in #2 (under the "Contribution amounts" section) can be made after year-end, but prior to your tax return deadline, including extensions. The contribution indicated as #1 must be made by year-end.
- **Contributions are not required**. You can contribute nothing or less than the maximum to the plan in any year and not be in violation of the plan.
- **Creditor protection**. The solo 401(k) is generally protected from the claims of creditors.

Disadvantages of A Solo 401(k)

As with everything, there are advantages and disadvantages. Be sure to consider these disadvantages before opening an account.

- **Set-up cost.** You will have a set-up cost to establish a solo 401(k) plan. You will also need a plan document and the appropriate filings are required. In addition, an investment account must be established. Sources for these services include banks, brokerage houses and independent financial institutions that can be accessed through the Internet. Generally, the cost for the establishment of the plan is $100 to $200.
- **Ongoing costs**. You will likely incur annual fees to cover any reporting or account maintenance. These fees generally range from $50 to $250 per year.

In summary, a solo 401(k) can provide a small business owner or sole proprietor with an enhanced means for saving for retirement, reducing income taxes and simplifying the management of multiple retirement plans through consolidation. As an added benefit, the solo 401(k) can also provide liquidity, if necessary, by allowing funds to be borrowed from the plan.

The solo 401(k) is one of several retirement plans that the sole proprietor or small business owner can use. The optimum plan will depend on income generated, ability to contribute to the plan and the cost of the plan administration. Therefore, it is recommended that you discuss your options with your tax advisor.

About Individual Retirement Accounts

Contributing to an IRA has real advantages. Here is a look at some options and a few facts about IRAs.

Contributions to an Individual Retirement Account (IRA)
Everyone with earned income (or a spouse with earned income) is able to make an annual contribution to an IRA. There are three choices: the deductible Traditional IRA, the non-deductible Traditional IRA and the Roth IRA. The maximum contribution to an IRA is indicated below. As a special incentive to those over age 50, the amount is increased by $500 and, later, by $1,000.

Year	50 and under	Over age 50
2005	$4,000	$4,500
2006	$4,000	$5,000
2007	$4,000	$5,000
2008	$5,000	$6,000

After 2008, the maximum contributions are scheduled to increase by $500 annually for those under age 50 and $1,000 for those over age 50. Contributions for the past year can be made any time before April 15 the following year.

Traditional IRAs

Here are the features that distinguish the Traditional IRA from the Roth IRA:

- Your contributions can be deductible or non-deductible.
- Your earnings are taxed when received.
- You must withdraw a minimum amount beginning at age 70 1/2 years.

For the Traditional IRA, the contribution is deductible on your income tax return if both you and your spouse do not participate in an employer-qualified retirement plan. An exception to this provision allows individuals within certain income levels to make a deductible contribution even though they participate in an employer plan. Those who do not qualify to deduct the IRA contribution can make a non-deductible contribution.

Once funds are in an IRA, the earnings accumulate on a tax-deferred basis. Taxation of any untaxed contribution or earnings occurs only when the funds are withdrawn. Distributions can be made without penalty beginning at age 59 ½ years. A minimum amount must be distributed beginning at age 70 ½ years.

Roth IRA

Here are the features that distinguish the Roth IRA from the Traditional IRA:

- Your contributions are non-deductible.
- Your earnings are tax-free.
- There is no requirement to withdraw at any age.

The Economic Growth and Tax Relief Reconciliation Act of 2001 created the Roth IRA. It allows for the accumulation of non-deductible annual contributions.

After the Roth IRA is held for a five-year period and you are at least 59 ½ years of age, your earnings are tax-free. You can contribute to the Roth IRA after age 70 ½ years as long as you have earned income. In addition, there is no minimum distribution from a Roth IRA.

At this time, the law also appears to allow the Roth IRA to be inherited by spouses and the next generation with the same tax-free characteristics.

In order to make a Roth IRA contribution, your modified adjusted gross income (AGI) must be less than $160,000 for married taxpayers (phase out begins at $150,000) or $110,000 for single taxpayers (phase out begins at $95,000). If you qualify, generally the Roth IRA will be more beneficial than the non-deductible Traditional IRA.

Conversion of Retirement Funds to Roth IRAs

If you have modified AGI under $100,000 (married and single taxpayers), you can convert existing Traditional IRAs into a Roth IRA. You will be required to pay any tax due on previously untaxed funds. Therefore, it is important that you consider the income tax impact as you determine the amount to convert. You can convert all or a portion of your Traditional IRA in any one year. You can convert additional amounts in any future year as long as you qualify based on your modified AGI.

Contribute To an IRA For Your Working Child

If your children have earned income from summer or part-time employment, they are eligible to contribute to an IRA. The maximum contribution may be limited by the amount earned. For example, if your son or daughter earned $2,250 in 2008, that is the maximum that he/she can contribute to the IRA even though the Internal Revenue Service limit is $5,000.

It is likely that a child can qualify for a deductible IRA. However, it may be more beneficial to utilize a Roth IRA. With only a limited amount of earnings, the child will pay little or no income tax. Making a non-deductible contribution to a Roth IRA will create a pool of funds earning tax-free for the rest of your child's life and perhaps his/her children's lives.

If your child or grandchild does not have the cash flow to make the contribution, you can make the eligible contribution to his or her Roth IRA. As long as your total gifts to the child or grandchild do not exceed $11,000 for the calendar year, you will not incur a gift-tax obligation. You will be investing for his/her future security as well as sending a message that saving is important.

IRA Beneficiaries

There is no federal or state law that requires you to name a specific person as beneficiary of your IRA. The owner of the IRA can name any person or entity as the beneficiary of his/her IRA. This includes a spouse, child, grandchild, non-related person, charity, trust or other entity. The income tax consequences and the required distribution rules may be different based on the beneficiary.

A bank, however, can establish such restrictions. The bank is serving as the "custodian" of the IRA. This means that the bank is required to hold the assets in an account and execute all the transactions. Such transactions would include buying and selling the investment vehicles and making the requested distributions. The custody duties can be provided by various institutions, such as a bank, broker or insurance company.

The custodian has the right to restrict the options offered through its IRA accounts. For example, it is common for the custodian to restrict the type of investment vehicles held in its IRAs. A bank may offer only certificates of deposit; a mutual fund company or broker may offer only its proprietary mutual funds.

Likewise, the custodian can restrict the options for the naming of the beneficiary. This may be due to the complicated distribution rules that apply with certain classes of beneficiaries. For example, if children were named as beneficiaries at the death of the owner, the

custodian would be obligated to make minimum distributions, which by law can continue for their expected lifetimes. This could be thirty or forty years. If grandchildren were named, the number of years would be even longer. Some custodians do not want to be obligated to perform such duties. Some custodians may allow children and grandchildren to be beneficiaries, but may restrict the distribution period to five or ten years instead of their expected lifetimes. For these reasons, a custodian may restrict the options for the naming of beneficiaries to those that are relatively simple, such as the spouse.

Check with your IRA custodian to assure that the institution can provide all the flexibility that you expect for your beneficiaries. If you are told there are restrictions, you should look for a different custodian. You can transfer your IRA account to a different custodian without tax implications.

Inappropriate Investments for Your IRA

As you accumulate your retirement nest egg, be aware of the investments you should avoid in your Individual Retirement Account (IRA). Some are illegal and others are just plain inappropriate.

IRA As a Source of Retirement Income

An IRA can play an important role in saving for retirement. Everyone who has earned income or a spouse with earned income can contribute to an IRA of some type each year. Your adjusted gross income will determine whether you are eligible for participation to a deductible or non-deductible Traditional IRA, or the Roth IRA. The greatest benefit of an IRA, regardless of type, is that your investments will grow tax-deferred.

You can establish an IRA with a bank, insurance company, brokerage firm or other qualifying financial institution. You are required to contribute cash. You cannot contribute real property or an investment you already own such as a mutual fund, stock or bond. All investments in the IRA must be purchased with cash deposited to the IRA account.

Illegal Investments

There are some investments that are prohibited by law for use in your IRA. These include items considered to be "collectibles" such as artwork, rugs, antiques, metals, gems, stamps, coins and alcoholic beverages. An exception exists for newly minted coins that are sold through the U.S. coin program, as well as some state-issued coins and certain bullion coins.

In addition, you cannot make loans to family members or any relatives from your IRA. This is considered a "prohibitive transaction."

Any dollars invested in collectibles or loaned to a relative are treated as an immediate distribution. You will be required to pay income tax on the amount and perhaps a 10-percent penalty if you are under age 59 ½ years.

Inappropriate Investments

There are several investments that are legal, but not appropriate for your IRA.

- **Municipal bonds**. As you may know, interest earned from municipal bonds is tax-exempt. Municipalities are able to issue bonds under a special provision that allows the interest paid to bond holders to be exempt from federal income tax. In addition, some municipal bond interest is also excluded from state and local income taxation. Since the income is tax-exempt, a lower interest rate for the bonds can be justified. Do not purchase municipal bonds for your IRA. All income distributed from an IRA is taxable, even if it is tax-exempt when earned. Therefore, you end up paying income tax on a lower municipal bond rate. The appropriate bond investment is the higher-interest bearing taxable government or corporate bonds.

- **Insurance annuity contracts**. An annuity issued by an insurance company is also an inappropriate investment for your IRA. One of the benefits of an annuity is that income earned by the underlying investments is tax-deferred. Just like the IRA, the annuity has a special provision that allows the income earned to be taxed only when withdrawn. An annuity investment in your IRA is putting a deferred product inside a deferred account. This is not illegal, but it is simply not a good use of your investment dollars.

  The annuity has multiple expenses associated with it. First, there are general administrative expenses charged by the insurance company to oversee the contract, provide annual reports, provide service to the policyholders, etc. Second, there may be an investment management expense charged if the annuity is invested in stock mutual funds or other equity investments. Third, since it is an insurance product, there is a "mortality expense." The mortality expense is a premium to pay for life insurance. The annuity contract includes a death benefit feature. The death benefit can be equal to the original contribution to the annuity contract or the value of the contract on specific dates, such as the anniversary date of the annuity purchase. At your death, if the annuity value, less any prior withdrawals, is less than the original contribution to the contract or the amount on the designated dates, the annuity will cash out at the higher amount. For this minimum value guarantee, you will pay a mortality cost based on your age and the amount that is being guaranteed or insured.

Since you do not need the "deferred income" feature of the annuity, the internal annuity costs make this an expensive investment for your IRA. You can invest in a fixed income vehicle or a stock mutual fund by simply purchasing those items directly in your IRA account much more efficiently.

- **Tax-oriented limited partnerships.** Ownership in a limited partnership whose primary purpose is to provide tax deductions is not appropriate for an IRA. The IRA does not pay tax, so a tax deduction is not used. Unfortunately, the tax deduction is never available to the owner of the IRA. It is wasted.

As you can surmise, the appropriate investments for your IRA include all the traditional vehicles such as certificates of deposit, taxable bonds, mutual funds and individual stocks. Incorporate these and other vehicles into your IRA investment plan based on the asset allocation appropriate for you.

Your IRA can enhance your retirement. Contribution limits to an IRA are increasing. The limits are scheduled to increase to $5,000 ($6,000 for those over age 50) by year 2008. Contribute and invest efficiently. If you start today and contribute $3,000 per year for 35 years, your account can grow to over $500,000, assuming an eight-percent annual growth rate.

What You Need to Know About Stock Options

Many employers provide stock options as part of an employee's compensation package or as a performance-based award. In a rising stock market, this form of compensation can be very lucrative. However, in a declining stock market, the employee may realize little or no value.

Stock options allow the employee to purchase shares of the company stock in the future at the price of the stock at the time the options are granted. It is a method of compensation and a means of providing an ownership interest to the employee.

There are two types of stock options, the "Non-Qualified Stock Option" (NQSO) and the "Incentive Stock Option" (ISO). Both types receive an exercise price equal to the current fair market value at the time of issue. Each will have a vesting date and termination date. However, the timing of the taxation of this benefit and the type of taxable income created is different.

Non-Qualified Stock Option

A Non-Qualified Stock Option is taxed at the time of exercise. Taxable income is created equal to the fair market value of the option at the time of exercise, less the exercise price. The income is taxed at ordinary tax rates at both the federal and state level. FICA and the Medicare tax are also applicable at the time of exercise.

Here is how taxation of a NQSO works. In this example, Pam receives 3000 NQSOs with an exercise price of $25.00 on July 14, 2003.

- **Vesting.** The stock option plan requires options to vest at a rate of 33.3 percent each year. Therefore, on or after July 14, 2004, Pam will be eligible to exercise 1000 of the stock options. Under this vesting schedule, another 1000 options will vest on July 14, 2005, and all options will be vested by July 14, 2006.

- **Stock price at exercise.** If the stock price increases above $25.00 per share, Pam's options have value. If the stock price decreases and is less than the exercise price of $25.00 per share, Pam would have no value. Such "worthless" options are sometimes referred to as "under water."
- **Stock price increases**. We will assume that the company stock price on July 14, 2004 is $30.00 per share and Pam decides to exercise the 1000 vested options. Pam will pay $25,000 ($25 times 1000) for 1000 shares of company stock that is worth $30,000 ($30 times 1000).
- **Income tax.** Pam will owe ordinary income tax on the value gained of $5000 ($30,000 less $25,000). Assuming a federal tax of 35 percent plus 4.1 percent state/local tax, Pam will pay $1,955 in income tax. FICA and the Medicare tax may also be owed.
- **Net benefit.** Pam will have a net investment benefit of $3,045 ($5,000 less $1,955). Pam can choose to either maintain the stock in her investment portfolio, or she can choose to sell some or all of the shares.

Incentive Stock Option

Incentive Stock Options are not taxed at the time of exercise as are Non-Qualified Stock Options. The taxable event for ISOs occurs at the time the stock received from the exercise is sold. If the stock is held for at least 12 months from the exercise date, the gain is taxed at the long-term capital gains rate of 15 percent. The exercise price is the basis value of the stock. If the stock is sold prior to the 12-month holding period, the short-term gain will be taxed at ordinary income tax rates.

Here is how taxation of an ISO works. In this example, Pam receives 3000 ISOs with an exercise price of $25.00 on July 14, 2003.

- **Vesting.** The stock option plan requires options to vest at a rate of 33.3 percent each year. Therefore, on or after July 14, 2004, Pam will be eligible to exercise 1000 of the stock options. Under this vesting schedule, another 1000 options will vest on July 14, 2005, and all options will be vested by July 14, 2006.
- **Stock price at exercise.** If the stock price increases above $25.00 per share, Pam's options have value. If the stock price decreases and is less than the exercise price of $25.00 per share, Pam would have no value. Such "worthless" options are sometimes referred to as "under water".
- **Stock price increases.** We will assume that the company stock price on July 14, 2004 is $30.00 per share and Pam decides to exercise the 1000 vested options. Pam will pay $25,000 ($25 times 1000) for 1000 shares of company stock that is worth $30,000 ($30 times 1000).
- **No tax at exercise.** Unlike the exercise of NQSOs, Pam owes no income tax at the time she exercises the ISOs.
- **Sale of stock.** Pam knows that she must hold the stock at least 12 months after the exercise date to take advantage of the beneficial taxation of the ISOs. We will assume that Pam owns the stock for three years and then sells all 1000 shares for $45 per share.
- **Capital gain tax at sale.** Pam has a long-term capital gain of $20 per share ($45 less exercise price of $25) or $20,000. She will owe $3,000 ($20,000 times 15 percent) in capital gain tax.
- **Net benefit.** Pam will have a net investment benefit of $17,000 ($20,000 less tax of $3000).
- **Alternative minimum tax.** There is one complicating factor. In the year that you exercise ISOs, you are required to include the difference between the fair market value and the exercise price as a preference item in the calculation of Alternative Minimum Tax (AMT). The AMT is a second calculation of your income tax. If the AMT calculation results in a larger tax than the regular tax

calculation, you owe the higher amount. Many individuals are subject to the AMT tax due to the exercise of ISOs. If possible, it is desirable to avoid the extra tax by using an exercise strategy that will offset the AMT. If you are required to pay the additional AMT tax, the additional amount can be used to offset the regular tax calculation in the year that the stock received from the ISO exercise is sold.

Timing of Stock Option Exercise

Timing is everything when it comes to exercising stock options. Here are some strategies to help you maximize your position.

- **Increasing stock price.** If the stock price is expected to increase in value equal to or in excess of the stock market, it is generally advantageous to hold options until just prior to the termination or expiration date. (Options generally expire 10 years from the initial grant date.) This allows you to maintain the cash that you would have used to exercise the options in another investment vehicle. Since the options receive the benefit of the stock price increasing, you, in essence, have two pools of funds invested instead of just one.
- **Decreasing stock price.** If the stock price is anticipated to decrease in value or to not increase at the level of the general stock market, it is advantageous to exercise as early as possible and immediately sell the stock.
- **Need to diversify.** An exception to the points made about increasing/decreasing stock prices occurs if there is a need to diversify your holdings to reduce exposure to the company stock. At the time of exercise of a NQSO, all tax currently due on the stock is paid. Therefore, immediately selling the stock and reinvesting the proceeds does not create an additional tax burden.
- **Additional consideration for ISOs.** Just as with NQSOs, when the company stock price is increasing, it is appropriate to hold the options until just prior to the termination or expiration date. However, because of the ATM issue, it may be advantageous to

exercise the ISOs over multiple years to avoid the extra tax. Due to the factors impacting this decision, you may want to seek advice from your financial planner or tax advisor.

Advantage of ISOs Versus NQSOs

ISOs are more advantageous for the employee than NQSOs for two reasons. First, any payment of income tax is deferred until the stock received in the exercise is sold. Second, the capital gain rate of 15 percent applies rather than the employee's ordinary income tax rate that can be as high as 35 percent.

Employer Stock in Your Qualified Plan: An alternative to rolling it over

Do you own your employer's stock in your 401(k)? If you are preparing to retire or "separate from service," you have an alternative means of handling it that may be more beneficial than rolling it into an IRA.

Special Tax Treatment of Employer Stock

Employer stock can be withdrawn from the qualified plan (401(k), pension or ESOP) at the time of separation from service. You pay ordinary income tax on the basis in the stock (the price paid for the stock when purchased in the plan). The difference between the basis and the fair market value of the stock on the date of distribution is referred to as the "net unrealized appreciation" (NUA). The NUA is taxed as long-term capital gain when the stock is sold, regardless of the holding period.

Eligibility Requirements

- You must be separating from service—either retiring or otherwise leaving the company.
- You must be receiving a lump sum from the retirement plan. This means that the entire account is being distributed by the employer, either to you or to an IRA Rollover account.
- You must not roll the stock into an IRA initially. The ability to use the special tax treatment is lost if the employer stock is first rolled into an IRA.

Special tax treatment may be advantageous or disadvantageous

Once you have established that you are eligible to use the special tax treatment, you need to determine if it is your best option. There are several factors or scenarios to consider.

- **Low basis**. The special tax treatment is only beneficial if the basis of the employer stock is relatively low given the current market value. If the majority of the employer stock was purchased recently or if the stock's value has declined, the special tax treatment would not yield a significant tax savings. In this case, the stock should be rolled into an IRA. Inside the IRA, the stock can be held or it can be sold and reinvested without tax consequences.
- **Need for liquidity**. The special tax treatment can be very beneficial if the plan participant needs funds immediately and his/her only resource is the qualified plan. For example, the participant may be leaving the employer and need funds to start a business or to meet living expenses. Even if the participant is under age 59 ½, the special tax cost plus the penalty may be less than paying ordinary income on IRA distributions.
- **Charitable gifting**. The low-basis stock would be an appropriate security to contribute directly to a charity or to a charitable re-

mainder trust. The participant would pay ordinary income tax on

the basis of the employer stock, but would avoid the capital gain tax on the NUA. In addition, the participant would receive a charitable deduction based on the fair market value of the stock.

- **High concentration of employer stock**. If you own significant shares of employer stock outside of the retirement account, it may be more advantageous to roll over the qualified plan stock into an IRA and diversify without tax consequence. Employees that receive stock options and stock grants may be in this situation. The over-weighting of the employer stock in the participant's overall investment portfolio may make the IRA Rollover the better alternative.
- **Lower tax rate in retirement**. If the participant expects to be in a lower tax rate in retirement, it may be more beneficial to roll over the qualified plan stock to the IRA and allow the continuation of the tax-deferred accumulation within the IRA. The participant may pay less tax overall by using the IRA Rollover for the employer stock.
- **Inherited IRA**. If the participant does not anticipate needing the proceeds from the employer stock, it may be better to allow the stock to rollover to the IRA. After the participant's death, the IRA beneficiaries will have the opportunity to continue the tax deferral over their lifetimes. This can be especially effective if the heirs are children or grandchildren.

How Does It Work?

For this example, we will assume that Sam is retiring. During the past 25 years of his employment, Sam has contributed to his 401(k). Along with other investments, he purchased his employer stock within the plan and the company's matching contributions also purchased stock. Of the total in Sam's 401(k), $150,000 is invested in employer stock. According to the company's records, over the years, Sam actually paid $35,000 for the stock that is now worth $150,000.

If Sam chooses to take advantage of the special tax treatment for employer stock, he would have the stock distributed to him and he would pay ordinary income tax on $35,000. If Sam sells the stock immediately, the NUA, or $115,000 ($150,000 minus $35,000), would be taxed as long-term capital gain at 15 percent. Sam can continue to own the stock and pay the long-term capital gain on the NUA when the stock is sold. Any additional gain would be taxed as long- or short-term gain, depending on the holding period from the date of distribution from the 401(k).

- Assuming a 35 percent marginal tax rate, Sam pays $12,250 ordinary income tax when the stock is received ($35,000 times 35 percent).
- At the 15 percent long-term, capital-gains rate, Sam will pay $17,500 on the NUA of $115,000.
- If Sam sells immediately, he would net $120,250 ($150,000 minus $12,250 minus $17,500).

If Sam is under the age of 59 ½ years and receives the company stock from the 401(k), he will be subject to the early-withdrawal penalty of 10 percent. The penalty would apply only to the basis in the stock. In our example, the 10-percent penalty would be an additional $3,500 ($35,000 times 10 percent).

Sam has the option of rolling over the employer stock to an IRA and avoiding any immediate taxation. However, when he withdraws the proceeds from the IRA, it will all be taxed at his ordinary income tax rate, which could be as high as 35 percent.

This special tax treatment is also available to beneficiaries of the qualified plan. In our example, if Sam had passed away prior to retiring, his beneficiary would be able to elect the special tax treatment for the employer stock.

The decision to use the special tax treatment for employer stock accumulated in your qualified plan will depend on many factors. Your anticipated future tax rate, liquidity needs and diversification concerns, along with your personal goals concerning charitable and family distributions, all need to be considered. Prior to making the election, you should discuss this option in detail with your personal financial planner or tax adviser.

Chapter 6

Family Affairs

Women and Money

Being single is not the only reason a woman needs to be attentive to her finances. Nearly every woman will find herself in total control of her finances or her family's finances at some point in her life. It is an inescapable fact of life. Why?

- **Women outlive men**. The average life expectancy for women is 79.8 years versus 74.4 years for men (National Center for Health Statistics, 2003). Seventy-five percent of married women become widows. While spouses often divide family responsibilities, with one taking the lead role when it comes to financial matters, it is still important for both spouses to have a general understanding of the financial picture and sufficient knowledge to act alone.
- **50 percent of marriages end in divorce.** The decisions made during the settlement negotiations greatly impact the future financial security of both parties. Women need to be aware of the family financial situation to make appropriate decisions.
- **Approximately 20 percent of women choose to remain single.** Independent women must rely on their own earning power and decision-making to meet current needs and future financial security.

Whether they choose the single life or not, according to the US Census Bureau, 54 percent of American women age 18 and older were unmarried and single in 2007.

Women Earn Less

According to the U.S. Census Bureau, on average, women earn approximately 75 cents for each dollar earned by men. Earning less money spills over into other areas of women's lives - fewer retirement benefits, lower Social Security benefits, less money from company pensions and less money to contribute to company savings plans or personal investment portfolios.

Women also tend to work part-time or leave the workforce to care for children or aging parents, which can impact their careers and earnings negatively.

The combination of living longer and accumulating less benefits has created a disproportionate number of women living in poverty. In 2006, 4.1 million households headed by women, with no husband present lived in poverty versus 671,000 households headed by men, with no wife present.

Women And Financial-Planning Issues

Women need to address all the following financial aspects of planning, taking into account individual needs, goals and strategies. The role a woman takes in life along with the prospect of living longer can impact various areas of planning.

- **Life insurance.** The purpose of life insurance is to meet the needs of dependents, replacing lost income and also services provided, something that is sometimes overlooked. Women who do not provide income to the family may need life insurance; women with no dependents may not.
- **Long-term care.** Women are more likely to need custodial care in their elder years. Studies indicate that 50 percent of women will utilize the services of a nursing home for some period of time after they retire, versus 33 percent of men.

- **Retirement planning.** The combination of lower earnings, interrupted careers and longer life expectancy often means women may need to work longer and save more to provide for retirement, making it even more important for them to start saving early in their careers.
- **Estate planning.** Women may procrastinate in this area, especially if they have no children. However, a will or trust document is the only means of assuring that favorite charities, family members or friends receive assets intended for them. Everyone needs a will to assure their assets are distributed according to their wishes.
- **Investment plans.** Women tend to consider and plan for the contingency needs of children and parents and, therefore, may have more money held in money market or other easily accessible funds. Given their longer life expectancy, women need to consider the impact of inflation on the purchasing power of their portfolio and plan accordingly.

Married women who choose to leave financial decisions solely to their husbands are at a disadvantage when they either divorce or become widowed. Single women who neglect money management often suffer in later years. It is important that all women develop money-management skills. Every decision concerning earning capacity, spending and investing, as well as a sudden change of events will impact future financial security. Just as important as being ready and able to make important financial decisions is the ability to understand when outside assistance and advice is needed.

Teach Kids to $ave, $pend and $hare

Parents generally provide the first and most lasting lessons on how to handle finances. Do you recall your first memories of money? Was it the pleasure of saving for a special purchase? Or was it the anxiety of never having enough? Recalling your feelings may help you understand the impressions your children are absorbing concerning money. Be proactive with your children in developing their money skills and you may discover that everyone enjoys and learns from the experience.

Successful money management is not a function of the amount, but rather the efficient allocation of the dollars between saving, spending and sharing. If you can instill these three principles, your children will have a good foundation for making future money decisions.

$ave. Teach your children to save half of the money they receive whether through gifts or their own earnings.

- Open a savings account for each child. Share statements with them or let them view the account over the Internet to encourage them to watch their money grow.
- Invest in an appropriate mutual fund once each child accumulates $500 or more.
- Teach children the "Rule of 72": Divide 72 by the fund's earning rate to determine the time required for their money to double. For example, at 8 percent their money will double in 9 years.
- When your child starts earning income, provide an added incentive to save by matching the amount he saves. Establish a Roth IRA in his name and contribute the eligible amount. Annual contributions of $1,000, beginning at age 15, will grow to over $570,000 by age 65, with an eight-percent annual return. If your child learns this "pay yourself first" lesson early and contributes the maximum each year, the amount can really accumulate.

$pend. A regular allowance for entertainment or special purchases is a good tool for teaching your child responsible spending.

- Introduce the concept of budgeting by having your child list anticipated purchases.
- Teach teenagers how to manage their spending by providing their allowance on a monthly, rather than weekly, basis. Extending the period of time as they get older helps them learn to manage their spending. You may want to consider providing an allowance for clothing, as well as entertainment. Be certain you and your children agree on the intended use for the funds.
- Allow children to make decisions concerning how they spend their money, but be prepared for mistakes! It is important that you do not bail your children out by lending them money or giving them their next allotment early. Let them suffer the consequences and pay the piper now while the stakes are not high.

$hare. Introduce the concept of sharing to children at an early age.

- Discuss having them save part of their weekly allowance for gifts for special occasions.
- Prepare a basket for a needy family during the holidays. Allow your children to use their own funds to purchase an item for the basket. Be sure they understand the appreciation expressed by the organization or family.
- Allow children to select an organization to receive a contribution in their name.

Monthly money lessons are available at Jump$tart Coalition, www.jumpstart.org. If you have teenagers, they may benefit from "Reality Check," a section geared specifically to them.

Money management is simply learning to save, spend and share responsibly. Remember, children will learn from your actions first and from your teachings second. Be sure both are on target!

Managing Family Finances During Uncertain Times

It happens. Companies eliminate positions and, regardless of your personal performance, you find yourself without a job. How do you prepare for such a situation? What can you do when it happens? The best time to consider these questions is while you have a job and the resources to put aside. Having a contingency plan in place will help you get through those lean times and experience a quicker recovery.

Preparing For The Possibility

As part of your financial plan, you should prepare for the potential loss of a wage earner's income. Whether the company closes, downsizes or reorganizes, the impact on you is the same. Take these steps now to help ease the hardship of reduced income when you are in-between jobs.

- **Maintain an emergency fund.** At all times, you should have enough money available in a savings or money-market account to cover three to six months of living expenses. You should also obtain a home equity line of credit now. If your job is terminated, you may not qualify. A line of credit can be a good source for funding in emergencies, but should not be used unless absolutely necessary.

- **Do not live paycheck-to-paycheck.** Maintain your lifestyle at a level that will allow you to save a specified amount from each paycheck. A good goal is to save 10 percent of each paycheck through your employer's retirement plan or your personal investment account. If you lose your job, you may have to stop saving, but your emergency fund and other resources will be able to meet your basic living expenses for a longer period of time. If your family has two wage earners, try to provide for all basic living expenses with one income. Then, if one person loses his/her job, the family can continue to meet its living expenses without a great deal of hardship.

- **Keep debt to a minimum.** The less debt you have, the easier it will be to adjust to a lower income. Your home mortgage and a car loan may be necessities, but personal or home equity loans to purchase luxury or "lifestyle" items should be avoided. It is better to save and purchase such items with cash. Manage your finances by tracking your cash flow and understanding where you can reduce or eliminate discretionary spending if it becomes necessary.

- **Pay off your credit card balance.** Always pay off your credit card balance when due. Then, as a last resort during your unemployment, you can use your credit card for the necessary items.

It Has Happened - Now What?

If you lose your job, you will need to make some immediate decisions concerning your employer's benefits and the family finances.

- **Severance payments.** You may receive a severance payment as either a lump sum or as a continuation of your paycheck for a period of time. If you receive a lump sum, it is important that you put it into your reserve fund to provide for future living expenses. Do not make the mistake of using it for a major "non-necessity" purchase, assuming you will quickly find a job.

- **Employer retirement savings plan.** You can roll over your 401(k) or other qualified employer savings plan to an IRA account. If you have an outstanding loan from your 401(k) plan, you will need to pay the loan off prior to the rollover. If you do not, you will be required to pay tax and/or penalty on the outstanding balance as if it were a distribution instead of a loan. Once your funds are in the IRA, you can withdraw money without a penalty for medical and education costs. Taxes, however, will still be owed on the withdrawals.

- **Medical Insurance.** You will lose your medical, dental and vision coverage provided by your employer. By law, you are eligible for COBRA coverage. This means you can stay in the company medical plan for a maximum period of eighteen months, allowing you to be covered temporarily while seeking other employment, but you are required to pay 100 percent of the costs. If your spouse is working, the first option may be to have the family covered under his/her employer plan. Your other option is to secure individual medical insurance, which is generally more expensive than an employer group plan. Unless you have no other choice, NEVER go without medical insurance.

- **Flexible spending plans.** Do not forget about the money you have in these accounts. Discuss with your employer the procedure for using any remaining pre-tax spending balance in your medical reimbursement or childcare accounts.
- **Job placement or training services.** Take advantage of any job placement or training programs that are available through your employer. The more you participate in the process, the greater the number of opportunities and the easier your search will be for a new position. Also, be sure to remain in contact with your former boss, colleagues and other business contacts.
- **Managing family finances during the job search.**
  If you have a two-income family and you have managed your finances well, you may have the luxury of being patient with your job search. If you have only one income and the other spouse is a "stay at home" parent, you may need to decide who has the greater potential for finding a position quickly. It may be advantageous to trade roles within the family for a period of time.

With a reduction in family income, you need to immediately control your spending. Develop a basic "bare bones" budget that will stretch your remaining income as far as possible. If you anticipate being without an income for longer than a few months, you may need to consider downsizing to reduce housing costs. Obviously, you will need to reduce or even eliminate any regular savings with the commitment to resume your savings habit when you have replaced the lost earnings.

You may also find it necessary to replace life insurance that was being provided by the employer. Life insurance represents security for your family in the event of your death. You should immediately consider a term policy to meet at least the minimum level of required coverage.

It should go without saying, but do not incur any new debt during this time unless it is absolutely necessary to meet basic living expenses! Look to your other sources for funds first, such as your emergency fund, the cash value in a life insurance policy or investments. If you must borrow money, consider a home equity loan.

Life Insurance: How much do I really need?

The main objective for owning life insurance is to assure that our dependents can continue to enjoy their lifestyle in the event of the loss of a family income earner. The younger you are, the larger the role life insurance may have in your financial plan. Calculating "how much" you need, determining "how long" you will need it and "what type" you need are important elements of your plan.

How Much?

When determining the amount of life insurance that is required to maintain your family's current lifestyle, you must consider both the immediate costs and the future needs. Use the following steps when calculating your need for life insurance:

1. **Immediate costs.** There may be costs associated with medical needs, memorial services and the transition period for the spouse and family. It would not be unusual for the immediate need to be $25,000 to $35,000.

2. **Debt elimination and education funding.** It is generally desirable to pay off the home mortgage and other loans to allow the spouse to be free of debt. In addition, setting aside the appropriate amount to fund a college education for each child can greatly reduce the future financial stress on the family. For this step, add up all outstanding loan balances and the lump sum needed today to provide for future college costs.

3. **Living needs.** A critical need of the family is the everyday funding of the expense budget. Start with the current annual expenses of the family. You can reduce this by the loan payments and education savings that have been satisfied in Step 2. In some cases, the remaining living expenses may be partially met by the spouse's after-tax earnings and/or Social Security payments that may be available for a time to both the children and the surviving spouse. With this information in hand, you want to calculate the lump sum necessary today to fund the future net

expenses. You need to consider the appropriate earnings and inflation rates, as well as changing situations, such as when the working spouse retires.

4. **Total funding need.** Add up the amounts calculated in Steps 1, 2 and 3. This amount represents the total funding necessary at your death to provide security for your family. If you have cash and investments equal to or greater than this required amount, you have met the family security need. If you have less than the required amount, you should purchase life insurance to make up the shortfall.

How Long?

The need for life insurance changes. Generally, a young couple with a mortgage and children have the greatest need for life insurance. The need for life insurance decreases as the mortgage is paid down, as the children finish college and become independent and as you accumulate investment assets over time. You can reasonably predict the mortgage payoff and the number of years until children become independent. Keep in mind, however, that it isn't uncommon for empty-nesters to still need life insurance to provide financial security for the surviving spouse until sufficient assets are accumulated to meet his/her needs.

What Type?

You may be able to acquire your life insurance through your employer's group plan. This is generally the least costly means of obtaining coverage. If this option is not available or is insufficient to meet your total need, you will need to consider purchasing life insurance that you personally own.

You can purchase two types of life insurance, term and permanent. A term policy provides only a death benefit. You can purchase an "annual renewable term" policy in which the premium costs increase each year, or every few years, to reflect the age of the insured. The older you are, the higher the premium. At some point, it will become cost prohibitive to continue owning this type of policy. You can also purchase a "level term" policy. A level term policy provides coverage for a predetermined period of years, usually 10, 15, 20 or 30 years. During the policy period the premium remains constant. A level term policy allows you to choose a policy that meets the period of need for your family.

A permanent life insurance policy combines a death benefit and a savings program. A portion of each premium is accumulated in the cash value account of the policy. The cash value is available for borrowing or withdrawing during the life of the policy. The permanent policy will stay in force as long as the premium is paid.

The premium for a permanent policy will be greater than the premium for a term policy with the same death benefit. A term policy is generally a better choice for a young family with limited cash flow.

Life insurance can be complicated. Estimate your need, do your own research on the Internet and consult with a qualified advisor, such as a CERTIFIED FINANCIAL PLANNER™ practitioner or an insurance professional.

Caring for Parents

The baby boom generation is often referred to as the "sandwich generation." While saving for their own retirement, baby boomers are sandwiched between putting children through college and caring for parents. What can you do if you find yourself caring for Mom and Dad?

Plan Ahead

The adult child that lives geographically closest to the parents' residence will likely be the one most involved in their care. Typically the first assistance needed is related to mobility. Elderly parents may be unable to drive due to physical ailments or the recognition of their inability to confidently maneuver in traffic situations.

It may also become necessary for adult children to participate in their parents' doctor appointments. The loss of a parent's ability to hear, understand and remember the conversations with the doctor may result in confusion about the prescribed medical treatment.

To be prepared for these situations, it is important that you have an understanding of your parents' desires and expectations for themselves as they grow older. This would include their living arrangements—i.e. remaining in their current residence, purchasing a maintenance-free condo or home or moving into a retirement living center. It also includes an assessment of financial resources to provide for medical and future custodial care. Reviewing these issues with your parents may allow for better planning now and better outcomes in the future.

Medical Care

Here are some items to consider as you maneuver through medical care issues for your parents.

- **Health insurance.** If your parent is over age 65 and participating in Medicare, does he/she have the appropriate Medicare supplement policy and Medicare Part D? Supplemental policies provide secondary coverage for services not funded by Medicare. Medicare Part D is a prescription drug policy. For all policies, the more benefits provided, the higher the premium. You may need to assist parents in filing the claims and tracking the reimbursements, which can be very time consuming.

- **Legal documents.** Two legal documents are very important: a living will and the appointment of a healthcare representative. The living will indicates the desires of the parent for life-sustaining measures in the event he/she becomes terminally ill. This document will relieve the children of the responsibility of making those decisions during a difficult time. The appointment of a healthcare representative will indicate to the physician and hospital the person who has the ability to make decisions on the part of the parent in the event that he/she cannot. In many cases this responsibility falls to the spouse and children. As with any legal document, it is important that the parents create and sign these documents while they possess full mental capacities.
- **Release of medical information.** In some cases it may be necessary for parents to sign a letter giving the doctor permission to discuss the parents' medical situation with the adult child. Given recent laws concerning the privacy of health information, this measure needs to be taken for the adult child to have the ability to call the physician with questions and issues.

Custodial Care

The financial situation of the parents may dictate the living arrangements once they become dependent on others for daily living needs. Generally the first choice is for the parents to remain in the home assisted by an adult child or a caregiver. Paying for a caregiver will become more and more expensive as the need increases from a few hours per day to twenty-four hours per day. If the finances are not available for a caretaker, the options become living with a family member or seeking a custodial care facility.

- **Long-term care insurance.** If your parents have purchased a long-term care policy, it is important that you know that it exists and understand the provisions. This policy may provide for home healthcare as well as custodial or nursing home costs. The home healthcare provision will pay for a non-family caregiver and, therefore, may allow your parents to remain at home. The policy will also provide a per-day amount to cover the expenses of living in a custodial care facility. The policy will provide these benefits for the number of years dictated by the policy or, if the lifetime provision was elected, for the entire time that the person needs home healthcare or lives in a nursing home. As with any insurance policy, the greater the benefits, the higher the premium costs. Another factor to consider is that the premium cost also increases with age, so buying a policy earlier, rather than later, may be a good strategy. Please note that premiums paid for a long-term care policy are deductible on Schedule A of the policy owner's federal income tax return.

- **Medicare.** It is important to understand that Medicare does not pay for ongoing custodial care in a nursing home. Medicare is a health insurance vehicle and not a long-term care policy. A limited amount of nursing home care is provided, as it relates to recovery from a medical condition after a related hospital stay. This does not include the need to have ongoing assistance to meet daily living needs.

- **Medicaid.** Medicaid is the welfare program provided by each State government for its citizens. It is meant to provide financial support for those individuals who do not have the resources to meet their living needs. Medicaid requires that individuals "spend down" the greatest portion of their assets in order to qualify for benefits. If an individual is in a nursing home and has exhausted all resources to pay for care, the Medicaid program will initiate financial assistance.

Impact on the Adult Child's Tax Planning

If you are providing a significant amount of financial support to your parents, you may be able to reduce the impact through tax deductions and spending pre-tax dollars.

- **Claiming your parent as a dependent.** If you provide more than one-half of your parents' financial support, you may be able to claim them as dependents on your income tax return. There are several requirements for claiming a dependent, so discuss this aspect with your tax accountant.
- **Dependent Care Reimbursement accounts.** If you are eligible to claim your parents as dependents, you can also utilize the Dependent Care Reimbursement account to pay for a limited amount of out-of-pocket expenses on a pre-tax basis. A Dependent Care Reimbursement account must be provided through your employer. Employees are eligible to contribute pre-tax dollars to this account and then claim reimbursement for the eligible expenses as incurred. This requires you to plan ahead since you must indicate your participation and the dollar amount prior to the beginning of the calendar year (usually in November for the following year). Generally employees utilize this account to pay for the childcare for their children while they work. It can also provide for the cost of adult day care for dependent parents as long as all the requirements to participate are met.

Providing financial assistance to your parents can impact the other two parts of the sandwich—saving for your children's college costs and planning for your own retirement. If you anticipate and desire to provide parental financial support, you should include this in your financial plan. The impact of doing so may mean postponing your own retirement or reducing your personal spending. Regardless, if you identify these issues as you go through the financial planning process, you will be able to review your options, make informed choices and better plan for your own future. It may even open your eyes to planning for your own care during your elder years.

Even Gift Cards Come With Instructions!

Gift cards are becoming a popular item during the holidays and throughout the year. 2004 expectations for holiday gift cards were that approximately 75 percent of consumers would purchase them, with the average shopper buying 3.4 cards valued at over $100. The holiday total was expected to exceed $15 billion, bringing the year's total gift card consumption to $40 billion.

People also like to *receive* gift cards. According to the National Retail Federation, 50.2% of those surveyed indicated gift cards were preferred to other gifts. Giving gift cards eliminates the decision on color, size and style for the giver and the need to stand in long lines to return an item for the receiver.

It may seem like an easy gift to give, but the instructions can get complicated. If you do not read the small print, the gift may dwindle or totally vanish over time.

Be An Informed Shopper

When you are shopping for a gift card, be sure you understand the "terms and conditions" and pass along this information to the recipient of the gift card. There are a variety of ways the card's value can be diminished.

Purchasing Fee

Before you purchase a gift card, be sure to ask whether a purchasing fee applies. Many gift cards issued by banks will tack on another $5.95 to $11.95 to the cost of the gift card. This means that a $25 gift card could cost as much as $30.95. This may cause you to reconsider and give cash instead!

Expiration Dates

Some gift cards may actually expire 12 to 24 months following the purchase date. You should alert the receiver of the gift card to this issue so he/she does not end up with a worthless card. This happened to about $2 billion worth of gift cards in 2003. Since the clock starts running at the date of purchase, you may need to communicate that date to the recipient as well. Early-bird shoppers may actually penalize the recipients of gift cards!

Dwindling Value

If a gift card remains unused or inactive for six months, it may begin to lose value at a rate of $1 to $2.50 per month. Some may even charge this fee retroactively. For example, let us assume the gift card that you purchase reduces in value by $2.50 per month after six months of no activity and that the charge is made retroactive to the purchase date. In this case, a $25 gift card would be worth only $10 after six months ($25 less $2.50 for each of six months) and worthless after ten months ($10 less $2.50 for each of four months). Again, the purchase date is important information to pass along.

Usage Restrictions

Some retail gift cards can be the most restrictive. Use may be restricted to only the specific store where they were purchased. Mall-issued gift cards are generally accepted at any store in that particular mall. Bank-issued gift cards are likely to be the most flexible, allowing use anywhere that particular bankcard is accepted. Another question to consider when buying gift cards: Can the gift card be used to purchase items on the Internet or through the mail? Sometimes the answer is "no".

Online Registration

You may want to register your gift card on the retailer's Web site if that service is provided. In the event that the card is lost or stolen, you may be able to get a replacement. You may also be able to check the card's remaining balance online. But be careful, a fee may be charged!

Chapter 7

All About Health

Who Will Make Health Care Decisions When You Are Unable?

What happens if you are unable to make your own health care decisions? By planning ahead, you can make your wishes known and name the individual that you trust to make such decisions on your behalf.

It is difficult for most people to consider a time when they cannot make decisions for themselves. Yet, this is exactly what happens when an accident or illness leaves us physically or mentally incapacitated and unable to either express our desires or logically evaluate our own medical situation.

The law allows you to officially express your desires as well as give permission to another person to make decisions concerning your health care when you cannot. There are two documents that you need to create: a living will and a durable power of attorney for health care (also called a Health Care Representative).

Living Will

A living will is a document that indicates your wishes concerning the use of life-sustaining medical treatment if you are terminally ill. In the event that you cannot express your desires, this document will address the use of life-support technologies, artificial nourishment, medication, pain management and the act of resuscitation.

The format and language used in the living will is determined by your state of residence. Since it is a legal document, you will want to use an attorney to draft your document or to review a living will that was created while you lived in another state to assure that it conforms to current state law.

Durable Power Of Attorney for Health Care

A durable power of attorney for health care allows you to name the person or persons that you would like to have serve as your health care representative(s) when you cannot make your own decisions. Unlike the living will, which applies only when you are terminally ill, your health care representative will make decisions concerning general health care issues when you cannot. For example, the health care representative may be required to make a decision concerning an unanticipated procedure in the middle of surgery. Other situations may involve treatment of an Alzheimer's patient or treatment for a person experiencing a period of unconsciousness due to an accident.

It is important to have the assistance of an attorney in drafting this document. You can be as explicit or as limiting as you would like in the document and, therefore, an attorney will be able to assure your desires are clearly understood and not open to interpretation.

Discuss Your Desires

It is very helpful to discuss the details of both the living will and the durable power of attorney for health care with family members, those that are named to represent you and your primary physician. In addition, you may want to write a letter of instruction that provides additional information or further expresses any concerns that you may have.

Where To Keep Your Documents

An original signed copy should be maintained in a safe but accessible place, such as a home safe or fireproof file cabinet. A safe deposit box is not a desirable location unless your representative has easy access to it.

Copies of the documents should be given to your health care representative and provided to your physician(s) for his/her office medical files. Most hospitals will request copies of these documents as part of the admitting process. Likewise, it will be important for the administrator of a retirement center or assisted-living facility to have a copy in his/her files.

Not Just For the Elderly

Since tragedy can strike at any time, it is appropriate for all adults, regardless of age or current health condition, to create and maintain these documents in advance of an unfortunate situation. You may be able to purchase "off the shelf" documents, but this is not advisable. Work with an attorney to draft and periodically review your documents to assure they comply with the current law and leave little room for interpretation.

Once you have these documents in place, you will feel more in control, and your family and friends will be in a better position to appropriately carry out your wishes.

Using Pre-Tax Dollars for Health Care

The cost of health care is increasing at a rate greater than inflation. What can you do? You may not be able to reduce the costs, but you can make your dollars go further by using a Medical Reimbursement Account.

Medical Reimbursement Account

A Medical Reimbursement Account is also referred to as a Medical Flexible Spending Account (FSA). If your employer provides this benefit, it is an opportunity for you to use pre-tax dollars to pay for your out-of-pocket medical expenses.

How Does It Work?

You must sign up to have money from each paycheck deposited into your Medical FSA during the October through December enrollment period when you make your other employee benefit selections. The IRS does not limit the amount you can contribute to your account. However, most employers limit the annual maximum contribution level to an amount in the range of $2,500 to $5,000.

Your contributions are not subject to income tax, so your dollars go into the account on a pre-tax basis. As you pay for medical services or medications that are not paid by your medical insurance plan, you can request reimbursement from your Medical FSA.

You never pay tax on the dollars received from your Medical FSA.

What Is The Benefit?

By using pre-tax dollars to pay for your medical expenses, you are significantly increasing your personal purchasing power. For example, if your dentist recommends your child have braces and your medical or dental plan does not cover the cost, you may have out-of-pocket expenses of $1,000 or more. Without a Medical FSA to fund the expense, you will need to earn $1,250 to pay the $1,000. This assumes a low federal tax rate of 15 percent and a state and local rate of five percent. If you are subject to a federal tax rate of 35 percent with an additional state/local tax of five percent, you would have to earn $1,666 to pay the $1,000 bill. Obviously, the higher your marginal tax rate, the greater the benefit. But even at the lower tax bracket you save $250 dollars for every $1,000 you must pay for medical costs!

What Is The Catch?

If you contribute more than you spend during the calendar year, your employer keeps the difference. This means you need to make a good estimate of your upcoming medical expenses. This is an excellent opportunity to reduce the cost of any elective medical procedures that can be scheduled for the next calendar year. Being conservative with your estimate may be best, but do not let the fear of losing money stop you from participating. The benefit on even a small amount of medical costs can be significant.

What Qualifies For Reimbursement?

The program originally limited out-of-pocket expenses to insurance plan deductibles and co-payments along with prescription drugs, eyeglasses, orthodontia and other physician ordered needs. Later the program was expanded to include over-the-counter medications such as pain relievers, cold medications, nicotine patches and bandages. Insurance premiums do not qualify for reimbursement and the company plan can restrict the list of reimbursable items. The addition of the non-prescription drugs has made the program even more attractive. The ability to stock up on over-the-counter medical supplies can reduce the risk of forfeiting the Medical FSA funds at the end of the year.

Take Advantage Of The Opportunity!

Medical expenses are continuing to increase at a rate greater than inflation. If your employer offers a Medical Reimbursement Account, do not miss the opportunity to participate. Unfortunately, according to a 2002 survey by Mercer Human Resource Consulting, only 18 percent of eligible workers take advantage of the opportunity to pay for medical expenses with pre-tax dollars. Take advantage. Sign up at the next opportunity.

Medicare Coverage

If you are age 65 or older, you are familiar with the medical insurance system provided by the government. For most seniors, Medicare coverage is by far the most affordable option for paying for healthcare costs. Medicare Part A is free, Medicare Part B is provided by the government at a cost and Medicare Supplement is the private insurance you purchase to manage the shortfall.

Medicare Insurance

The U. S. Government provides Medicare coverage to all citizens age 65 or older who are eligible, based on their earnings record as maintained by the Social Security System. The spouse of any eligible worker is also provided Medicare benefits. Those under age 65 years who are disabled or have a specific need, such as kidney dialysis, are eligible to be covered by the Medicare system as well.

There are two parts to Medicare coverage:

- **Part A**. This part of Medicare coverage is free, and any eligible person attaining the age of 65 is automatically signed up. Part A will pay for hospital expenses only. It does not pay for routine doctor visits, lab tests or other medical related costs.
- **Part B**. Participation in Medicare Part B is voluntary and requires the payment of a fee, which is deducted each month from your Social Security payment. Just like all medical costs, the monthly fee for Medicare Part B is also increasing. The monthly cost is adjusted annually. An eligible individual can sign up for Medicare Part B as early as three months prior to age 65, but it is not effective until age 65. Medicare Part B covers 80 percent of non-hospital costs, such as doctor appointments, tests and x-rays, some medical equipment, outpatient surgery, physical therapy and ambulance services. Some preventative expenses such as flu and pneumonia shots, diagnostic exams such as colonoscopies, mammograms and PSA tests, and nutrition therapy, podiatry and chiropractic care are cover by Medicare Part B.

However, Part B does not pay for dental, hearing or vision needs. It also does not pay for nursing home care (except for a limited time for rehabilitation after a hospital stay) or custodial care in your home. It is important to note that medical needs outside of the United States are not covered by Medicare.

Medicare Supplement Policy

Since Medicare Part A and Part B do not cover 100 percent of the costs of medical care, you should purchase a Medicare supplement policy (also referred to as Medigap coverage). The insurance industry regulators have required each company offering this type of coverage to be uniform in their offerings. Plans are labeled A through J. All insurance companies that offer "A" plans are required to provide the same standard of coverage within the plan as any other insurance company offering an "A" plan. The same applies to plans B through J. This makes it much easier for you to compare policies among insurance companies when making your buying decisions.

Medigap coverage takes care of the 20 percent of the medical costs that Medicare Part B does not pay. A Medigap policy can be purchased the month of the individual's 65th birthday. The "open enrollment" period extends for six months from age 65. During this period, an applicant cannot be denied coverage or have restrictions or increased costs placed on the policy due to health problems. Therefore, based on the applicant's condition of health, it may be important to purchase this coverage before age 65 and 6 months.

Medicare Part D is a partially subsidized Medicare prescription drug payment plan offered by third-party providers to anyone over age 65. Coverage and costs vary according to each plan. Part D has detailed rules regarding health plans provided by former employers and set enrollment periods. Participation in the right plan may result in significant savings for you, but you will need to investigate all plans offered in your state to find the best one for you.

Purchasing Coverage

The only reason to not take advantage of the Medicare system is if you have coverage provided by an employer or your spouse's employer that does not cost as much as Medicare Part B combined with the Medigap insurance. However, you do run the risk of being "rated" for coverage if you apply for a Medicare supplement policy after age 65 and 6 months for Part B and you have a health problem.

The cost of medical care is increasing each year. The Medicare coverage provided by the government is not a perfect system, but it does provide coverage for most health care needs at a reasonable price.

Do I Need Long-Term Care Insurance?

The fastest growing sector of our society is individuals aged 65 or older. According to recent research, 70 percent of the over-65 population will need some form of long-term care. Ninety percent of long-term care services are custodial, with assistance provided for daily activities. Medicare does not pay for custodial services.

Since most individuals over age 65 use home health care for 4.5 years on average before entering a nursing home, it is important that a long-term policy provide both home health care and nursing home benefits. Round-the-clock home health care can cost three times as much as nursing home costs for the same time period.

The cost of nursing home care will vary based on your geographic location and availability of services. The average stay is 2.5 years; however, we all know of individuals who spend 10 or more years in a care facility.

Health care plans and Medicare combined generally provide only three percent of the cost of long-term care. The additional cost is typically funded through individual investments and other family assets, proceeds from a long-term care policy, or a state's Medicaid program. Medicaid is available after assets are depleted to a minimum amount set by your state of residence.

Your Choice: Self-Insure Or Purchase A Policy

If you have sufficient savings, providing for the expenses of long-term care through your cash flow and investment assets may be a viable option. Generally, families with assets in excess of $2,000,000 can self-insure.

If you have assets in the range of $1,000,000 to $2,000,000, you may want to consider purchasing a policy. Senior couples with this level of assets would likely spend all the funds in the event both spouses needed such care. However, you should consider the likelihood of the healthy spouse caring for the ill or disabled spouse in their home. If you have limited assets, the cost of a policy may be prohibitive. You may consider a policy that provides a limited benefit that will supplement your other assets. Medicaid may be the only alternative if there is a prolonged need for this type of care.

Do Your Research

Multiple financial factors need to be considered when determining your need for a long-term care policy. In addition, your personal desire to preserve assets for your heirs may influence your decision.

If you decide to purchase a policy, you will need to do your homework. There are multiple policy features to review. The state of Indiana also provides an incentive you may want to investigate. Refer to "Long-Term Care Insurance and the Indiana Incentive" for more information.

The Indiana Long-Term Care Insurance Program and the Indiana Incentive

The state of Indiana provides an incentive for individuals to purchase a long-term care policy. If you purchase a policy that qualifies under the Indiana Long-Term Care Insurance Program (ILTCIP), you can protect your assets from the required Medicaid "spend down" once the benefits under the policy are exhausted. These policies are known as "Partnership policies."

Medicaid Program

The state government administers the Medicaid program, a welfare system that is meant to assist individuals who do not have the financial means to provide for their own care. It is the state Medicaid program, and not the federal Medicare program, that provides funding for nursing home care to those who qualify. The state of Indiana establishes the requirements for Indiana residents to qualify for its Medicaid program. To receive funding for nursing home care, you and your spouse are required to "spend down" your assets to a certain level. This required "spend down" will often leave the healthy spouse with few assets to provide for his/her own future needs.

Partnership Policies

The ILTCIP is a public-private partnership between the public Medicaid office and private long-term care insurance companies. To encourage individuals to plan for their long-term care needs, the state of Indiana provides an incentive. For each dollar of long-term care benefit provided by a Partnership policy, a dollar of assets is protected from spend down. For example, if you purchase a policy providing $100,000 of benefits and you utilize those benefits, you can apply immediately for Medicaid. To qualify for Medicaid you will need to spend down your assets to $100,000. The $100,000 is protected and will remain in your estate regardless of the continued benefits received from Medicaid.

A Partnership policy allows you to protect all of your assets from the required Medicaid spend down if you purchase a minimum amount of coverage. The following table illustrates the required amounts based on the initial policy purchase year:

2006	$206,844
2007	$217,186
2008	$228,045
2009	$239,449
2010	$251,419

For example:
If you purchase a long-term care policy in the year 2008 that provides benefits equal to $228,045, once those benefits are exhausted, you can apply for Medicaid and all your assets are protected.

A Partnership policy protects assets, but not income. Therefore, Medicaid would take into consideration the income you receive when determining whether you qualify for Medicaid benefits. Income includes interest and dividends, whether taken directly or reinvested. It also includes Social Security benefits and pension payments.

What happens if you move to Florida and enter a care facility in that state? A policy that qualifies for the Indiana Partnership Program will provide benefits to the nursing home facility in any state. However, the state of Florida will require you to "spend down" your assets to their required level prior to receiving benefits from the Florida Medicaid system. You need to be in Indiana to reap the benefits of the Partnership policy. Therefore, even though your policy benefits were spent in another state, if you move back to Indiana, you will resume the original partnership benefits and will qualify immediately for Medicaid. For additional information, you can log on to the Indiana Partnership Program Web site at http://www.in.gov/fssa/.

In summary, if you decide to purchase a long-term care policy and expect to spend your retirement years as an Indiana resident, you should purchase a Partnership policy. To qualify, the policy must include certain features. However, qualifying does not increase the cost. The policy would be comparable in price to any policy with the same features.

Chapter 8

Retirement Considerations

Retirement: Is it an option for you now?

You may be ready and willing, but are you financially able to retire now? To answer this question, you need to understand your sources of income and determine your anticipated living expenses.

Sources of Income in Retirement

Many of us consider the three-legged stool when we assess our funds in retirement. We look to three sources: employer-provided pension or savings plan, Social Security and our personal savings. The first two legs of the stool, employer-provided funding and Social Security, are unique to each individual. The employer plan may provide a guaranteed payment from the employer to you and/or a savings plan that requires a contribution from your salary and may also receive a contribution from the employer. Your Social Security payment is based on your work career (longevity and earnings). Once the payment is determined, it stays relatively the same, adjusting only to reflect the annual cost of living. The third leg, personal savings, becomes the balancing factor for the three-legged stool. It is generally your personal savings that determines your lifestyle in retirement.

Living Expenses in Retirement

You may have an idea of your anticipated expenses during retirement. If not, a good place to start is with the amount you are spending today. Adjust this amount by subtracting work-related and other expenses that will not continue in retirement, and by adding expenses for retirement activities, such as travel. Unfortunately, it may also be necessary to consider the extra costs for health insurance and out-of-pocket medical expenses. Be sure to adjust this amount to reflect the payment of income taxes.

Personal Savings Required

Once you have determined the amount you will need, subtract the employer-provided pension and Social Security benefits. (Check your annual statement from Social Security for the expected payment.) The remaining amount needs to come from your personal savings. The following chart may help you approximate what you will need in your personal investment portfolio.

Assumption: 3% annual inflation and 8% annual investment return.

Annual Payment From

Personal Savings:	$25,000	$50,000	$100,000
Payment Period:			
20 years	$325,000	$650,000	$1,300,000
25 years	$465,000	$730,000	$1,460,000
30 years	$400,000	$800,000	$1,600,000

For example:

If you want to continue your annual taxable income of $50,000, and you receive $12,000 per year from Social Security and $13,000 from your employer pension or savings plan, you would need an additional $25,000 annually from your investment portfolio. This means that you will need an investment portfolio of $325,000 if you retire at age 65 years and live to 85 years. You will need additional funds if you want 25 or 30 years of financial security.

In addition to pen-and-paper calculations, there are many on-line retirement calculators that can help you assess your readiness for retirement.

Decision Time

If your calculations show you have a shortfall, you have three options.

- Spend less and save more to accumulate enough portfolio assets.
- Delay your retirement and work longer.
- Reduce your expectations for spending in retirement.

Now you have a good basis from which to make your retirement decision. Will it be now or later?

Spending Wisely During Retirement Years

In retirement, the focus shifts from saving money for retirement to spending the money you have accumulated for just that purpose. Knowing how to spend those funds wisely is essential.

Non-Retirement Funds

Accumulating funds for retirement in your personal investment portfolio is generally necessary to complement your Social Security and company retirement benefits. Each year, you are required to pay income tax on interest, dividends or realized capital gains that accumulate in your non-retirement portfolio. Therefore, using funds from your non-retirement accounts does not create additional taxable income. It is more tax-efficient to utilize your non-retirement funds *before* your retirement accounts, since each withdrawal from a retirement account creates taxable income. The general rule is to spend down all non-retirement funds before your retirement funds.

Investment Earnings Versus Principle

Many retirees attempt to accumulate sufficient investment assets to allow them to spend only earned income and not principal during retirement. While this appears to be a solid concept that provides the comfort that the portfolio will never be depleted, it is not the most tax-efficient means of handling your non-retirement and retirement accounts. It is more tax-efficient to allow your earnings to stay in your retirement account and continue to earn tax-deferred income rather than creating taxable income with the withdrawal. Both the earnings and principal should be used in the non-retirement portfolio until it is depleted. Then the retirement accounts should be used.

Lower Tax Brackets

Many retirees will experience low taxable income in the early years of retirement, especially if they are not receiving a company pension and are spending from their non-retirement accounts. If you are in this situation, you may have an opportunity to reduce the overall tax paid on your retirement investments if you anticipate paying tax in one of the higher brackets when withdrawals from your retirement accounts begin. To take advantage of this opportunity, you (the retiree) should estimate your taxable income in November or December. Withdraw, prior to year-end, the amount from your retirement accounts that will allow you to use the lowest two or three tax brackets. This exception to the general rule of depleting non-retirement funds first will allow you to reduce the overall tax assessed on your retirement funds.

Combine Your Retirement Accounts And Simplify Your Life

Do you have multiple IRAs? Do you have an inactive 401(k) or SEP IRA? Combining these accounts into one IRA can save you time as well as storage space. It may even improve your investment performance!

Individual Retirement Accounts

If you are a typical investor, you likely have three or four different retirement accounts. This is not necessary. You can open an IRA with a discount broker, such as Schwab or Fidelity, and purchase mutual funds from different fund families within the same account. You may have to pay a transaction fee to make the purchase, but you will reduce the number of annual account fees that are generally required by each custodian. You may or may not save money, but you will have only one statement to review and file each quarter!

All deductible and non-deductible traditional IRAs can be combined. The exception is a Roth IRA. You cannot consolidate funds from a Roth IRA with a traditional IRA. These accounts must remain separate.

Employer Retirement Plans

It is also very common for people to allow their retirement funds to remain in their employer plans, such as a 401(k), 403(b) or pension plan, after leaving the employer. But these funds can be rolled over to an IRA as well. Since company plans typically offer only a limited number of investment options, you increase your investment selection while reducing the number of accounts.

If you return to the workforce after your initial retirement, another alternative is to roll your previous employer's retirement plan into your current employer's plan. The advantage of this strategy is to allow you to borrow funds from the account in the future, if necessary. You can borrow money from an employer 401(k) or 403(b) plan, but you cannot borrow from your IRA account. This is an important consideration. However, if you have no intention of borrowing from your plan, then the IRA rollover would provide more investment flexibility.

Beneficiary distribution options are another reason to consider rolling the funds from a past employer plan to an IRA. The company may limit the options for distribution to your heirs if the funds remain in the plan. The IRA will provide maximum flexibility for distributing funds to heirs of your choice in the most tax-advantaged method.

Self-Employed Plans

If you are self-employed or have been at any time in the past, you may have established a self-employed plan such as a Simplified Employer Plan (SEP) or Keogh plan. If you are no longer making contributions to the plan, it is considered "inactive." An inactive plan can be rolled into your existing IRA. You may need to have the appropriate paperwork filed to officially terminate some plans, while others, such as an SEP, do not require official termination. Likewise, if you have employees in the "inactive" plan, you must be careful to distribute their share in the appropriate manner. Your plan administrator can assist you.

Retirees Over Age 70

In the past, it was advantageous to create multiple IRAs prior to age 70 ½ if you had multiple beneficiaries and wanted to provide greater flexibility, but it is now possible for retirees over 70 ½ years of age to maintain one IRA and still have multiple beneficiaries.

Minimum distributions must be taken from your traditional IRA accounts beginning in the year you become 70 ½ years of age. (Minimum distributions are not required from Roth IRAs.) Combining IRA accounts will make the calculation and the distribution of the minimum amount much easier.

Investments to Avoid

When you open a new IRA, steer clear of inappropriate investments, such as municipal bonds, insurance annuity contracts or tax-oriented limited partnerships.

- **Municipal bonds.** Interest earned from municipal bonds is tax-exempt and generally has a lower interest rate. However, all income distributed from an IRA is taxable, even if it is tax-exempt when earned. Therefore you end up paying income tax on a lower municipal bond rate.
- **Insurance annuity contracts.** One of the benefits of an annuity is that income earned by the underlying investments is tax-deferred. An annuity investment in your IRA is putting a deferred product inside a deferred account. Due to the added expenses incurred with an annuity product, it is simply not a good use of your investment dollars.
- **Tax-oriented limited partnerships.** Ownership in a limited partnership, with a primary purpose of providing tax deductions, is not appropriate for an IRA. The IRA does not pay tax, so a tax deduction is not used. It is wasted!

More Incentives

Here are some additional benefits to be gained from combining your retirement accounts:

- Reduces the number of account statements received and filed.
- Eliminates costs associated with multiple custodian fees.
- Provides a broader investment selection.
- Eases the tracking of your portfolio performance.
- Simplifies calculation of minimum distributions.

Combining your IRAs will take a little time initially, but the benefits are well worth it.

Making Sense of Minimum Distributions

The Internal Revenue Service (IRS) requires you to withdraw a minimum amount from your retirement accounts beginning in the year you attain 70 ½ years of age. Prior to that year, you may withdraw as little or as much as you like without penalty, as long as you are at least 59 ½ years of age. The penalty for an insufficient withdrawal is hefty—50 percent of the required minimum distribution.

Here is how the minimum distribution process works. Your first year's required distribution may be deferred to the year following the year you turn 70 ½, but must be received prior to April 1 of that year. You will be required to take a second distribution in that same year, but this strategy allows you to defer the income to the following year for tax purposes.

Calculating Your Minimum Distribution

The accumulated value of all your retirement accounts is subject to the minimum distribution calculation and is based on a uniform lifetime table published by the IRS.

Here are the steps:

1. Determine the total value of all your retirement accounts as of December 31 of the previous year. If you have combined your retirement accounts into one IRA, calculating the minimum distribution amount is much easier. Refer to "Combine Your Retirement Accounts and Simplify Your Life" if you have multiple IRA or other retirement accounts.
2. Divide that total value by the factor from the Minimum Distribution Factor Table, based on your (the retiree) birth date age in the calendar year. There is only one exception: If your spouse is more than 10 years younger than you are, then the IRS provides a different factor table and the result will be that a lesser amount can be withdrawn.

3. Distribute at least the amount from your calculation in Step 2 from your retirement accounts prior to December 31. You can take the amount early or late in the year, as long as it is all distributed before year-end. You can take the total amount at one time or as multiple distributions throughout the year and you can take the total amount from several accounts or all from one account.

4. Repeat Steps 1 through 3 for each future year.

Minimum distribution amounts are simple to calculate and take just a few minutes each year, especially if you have combined your IRAs. Calculate your minimum distribution as soon as you receive the account value information from the last calendar year and schedule your withdrawals appropriately so you meet the requirement. Paying penalties unnecessarily is not the way to stretch your retirement dollars.

Minimum Distribution Factor Table

Age	Factor	Age	Factor	Age	Factor
70	27.4	85	14.8	100	6.3
71	26.5	86	14.1	101	5.9
72	25.6	87	13.4	102	5.5
73	24.7	88	12.7	103	5.2
74	23.8	89	12	104	4.9
75	22.9	90	11.4	105	4.5
76	22	91	10.8	106	4.2
77	21.2	92	10.2	107	3.9
78	20.3	93	9.6	108	3.7
79	19.5	94	9.1	109	3.4
80	18.7	95	8.6	110	3.1
81	17.9	96	8.1	111	2.9
82	17.1	97	7.6	112	2.6
83	16.3	98	7.1	113	2.4
84	15.5	99	6.7	114	2.1

Source: Internal Revenue Service

Which Pension Benefit Should I Take?

If your employer offers a "defined-benefit" retirement plan (payment is based on factors such as years of service or salary rather than on investment performance) you will be faced with some decisions as you approach retirement. Should you take a lump-sum distribution or a monthly pension? If the lump-sum distribution is not an option, you have to decide between taking the full monthly amount available (full single-life benefit), which provides no benefit to the surviving spouse, or taking a reduced amount that provides an ongoing benefit to the spouse after the retiree's death. There are advantages and disadvantages to each choice. Determining the right decision for you may require some number crunching.

The Lump-Sum Distribution and The Monthly Pension

An interest rate, based on a combination of the U.S. Treasury bill rate and corporate bond rates, is used to calculate the lump-sum dollar amount that is equivalent to the monthly pension. Eventually, only a corporate bond interest rate will be used in determining the lump-sum amount. The lower the applicable interest rate used in the calculation, the larger the lump-sum amount. In a changing interest-rate environment, the lump-sum amount can change significantly over a period of a few months. If you are approaching retirement, it is important to take the interest rate under consideration when choosing your actual retirement date.

There are several advantages to taking the lump sum. The lump sum can be rolled over into an Individual Retirement Account (IRA), where the funds can be held and invested until needed. This flexibility can allow the lump sum to continue to grow tax-deferred while other resources are used to meet your needs. Since you only pay tax on the funds when withdrawn, you have the opportunity to control your taxable income each year. The lump-sum option also allows you to withdraw, when needed, an amount greater than the monthly pension amount alternative for larger expenditures. One of the greatest benefits of the lump sum is the ability to allow your heirs to inherit any unused funds.

The responsibility that comes with selecting the lump-sum distribution is investing the funds wisely. Doing so can increase the overall benefit of the lump-sum distribution over the pension. The other responsibility is controlling the temptation to utilize all the funds in the early years of retirement. If you question your ability to control the withdrawals, the pension may be the better option. By far, the greatest advantage of the monthly pension is that the payment is guaranteed for your lifetime.

Full Single-Life Benefit or Reduced (Spousal) Benefit

If you (the retiree) select the reduced benefit and you predecease your spouse, your spouse is guaranteed a continuing stream of income for his or her lifetime. You will have the benefit of knowing that your spouse will not outlive this source. If there are no other sources of income or family assets available to meet your spouse's living expenses, or if they are not as reliable or may be depleted, choosing the spousal option may be the best decision.

Choosing a spousal option, however, will reduce the amount of funds available to you and your spouse during your lifetime. This may require spending down other assets to meet living expenses. Choosing a spousal option may mean the family will never realize the full financial benefit if the pensioner does not live to his or her full life expectancy, regardless of who predeceases.

The decision would be very easy if you could determine which spouse will outlive the other. Without this knowledge, the decision is between financial security for the spouse and receiving the full retirement benefit.

A Strategy to Consider

An often-considered strategy is to take the full single-life benefit and purchase life insurance to replace the pension payment, or some portion of it, for the surviving spouse.

There are two major concerns with this strategy. One is maintaining the policy. If money became tight, the policy might be terminated, leaving the spouse without the necessary funds to replace the pension. The second is managing the life insurance proceeds. There is a risk of investment performance and a risk of spending down the funds too quickly.

When you make your decision, be sure to consider family assets and the other sources of income for both spouses. In addition, health concerns may be an influencing factor. If your decision is not clear-cut, consult a qualified adviser.

Is My Pension Guaranteed?

It is an unfortunate consequence of today's business climate that companies declare bankruptcy, putting the retirement security of their employees and retirees in jeopardy. The Pension Benefit Guaranty Corporation (PBGC) guarantees the pensions of some companies that declare bankruptcy. However, the amount of coverage depends on the person's age, type of benefits and other factors beyond the control of the employee or retiree.

Pension Benefit Guaranty Corporation

PBGC was created in 1974 by the Employee Retirement Income Security Act (ERISA). The program includes only defined benefit plans, i.e. plans designed to pay a specific monthly amount to retirees. Other employer retirement plans, such as 401(k) and profit-sharing plans, are not included in the coverage. It is also important to note that only basic pension benefits are included. Any supplemental pension plans provided by the employer are not included.

PBGC covers most employers who offer defined-benefit plans. Employers that are usually not covered include professional practices (doctors, lawyers, accountants, etc.) with fewer than 26 employees, church groups and federal, state and local governments. Review the "Summary Plan Description" that is provided by your employer to determine whether your plan is included in the PBGC program. If it is not covered, you should realize that your future benefits are based solely on your employer's ability to pay.

Employers of covered plans pay an insurance premium to PBGC. These funds, along with investment earnings and assets of the bankrupt company pension plan, are used to pay benefits to individuals. The PBGC funding includes no tax revenue.

What Does PBGC Provide?

Unfortunately, PBGC may not cover the entire amount of your earned monthly pension. There are maximums established. *For example, in 2007, the maximum coverage available for a 65-year-old was $4,125 per month ($49,500 per year).* This means that anyone age 65 that received more than this amount from their employer plan was not fully covered in the event of the company's bankruptcy. For younger participants, the maximum covered amount is smaller. For older participants, the amount is larger. A table of the monthly maximum guarantees is provided on PBGC's Web site at www.pbgc.gov. These amounts are increased each year to compensate for inflation.

Is Your Pension In Jeopardy?

To determine whether your pension is in jeopardy, you need to understand the financial strength of your employer. You can determine this by reviewing the company's annual report. The company's credit rating is also an indication of the ability for the company to pay its debts.

You should also review the "Summary Annual Report" that the company is required to provide to each pension participant. This report will indicate the assets and level of funding of the pension plan. Your employer is also required by law to provide each covered employee, upon request, an individual benefit statement and summary plan document. This should allow you to determine the amount of your accrued benefit and the formula for calculating your future benefit. Once your benefit is known, you can determine whether the PBGC insurance will cover all, or only a portion, of the amount.

Take Control of Your Situation

If your company is in bankruptcy, there is little you can do. If the company is showing signs of declining financial stability, an organized employee group may be able to persuade management to contribute to the pension funds in lieu of other expenditures, but it is doubtful.

The best way to protect yourself is to understand your personal situation and make decisions that allow you to guarantee your own financial security. If your pension is in jeopardy, it may be wise for you to consider finding a new employer who is financially secure. If you determine you may not receive the pension that you are counting on in retirement, you may need to start saving more of your paycheck for future expenses.

Social Security Retirement Benefits

A common question asked by those approaching retirement is when to begin receiving Social Security benefits. Retirement benefits from Social Security can begin at age 62, but is the reduction worth it?

The decision regarding when to begin receiving Social Security depends on two factors: When you plan to stop earning income and your anticipated longevity.

Full Retirement Age

If you begin receiving benefits from Social Security as early as age 62, the amount you receive will be less than the amount you would receive if you waited until your full retirement age. Surprisingly, age 65 is no longer the age at which full benefits are received. Individuals turning age 65 in 2008 (born in year 1943) will have to wait until they are 66 to be eligible for full benefits. Year 2003 was the first year in which individuals did not reach full retirement age on their 65th birthday (anyone born in 1938). Full Social Security benefits became available for this group at 65 years and 2 months. For each birth year thereafter until 1943, two additional months are required before qualifying for full benefits, i.e. those born in 1939 must be 65 and 4 months, those born in 1940 must be 65 and 6 months and so on. Individuals born in years 1943 through 1954 must be 66 years before they reach full retirement age. For each birth year thereafter until 1959, two additional months are required before qualifying for full benefits. Those born in 1960 and later must be 67 years of age. Regardless of when you reach your full retirement benefit age, you can still receive a reduced benefit as early as age 62.

No Earned Income Expected

If you are 62 years or older and no longer have earned income, you should consider applying for Social Security benefits. The reduction is .525% from the full retirement amount for each month you start receiving benefits early. For example, those turning 62 in 2008 (born in 1946) would reach full retirement at age 66.

Receiving benefits 48 months early would result in a benefit reduction of slightly more than 25 percent. Even though you will receive a reduced amount at age 62 versus your full retirement age, it generally takes 11 to 12 years to break even.

Break-Even Calculation

To calculate the break-even point, divide the total amount that you would receive during the years prior to your full retirement age by the incremental increase in your monthly benefit at your full retirement age. The result is the number of months to reach your break-even point.

> ***For example:***
> *Let us assume you would receive $1,000 per month at age 66 (full retirement age). Given the reduction explained above, at age 62 you would receive approximately $750 per month. For the four years (age 62 to 66) that you receive $750 per month, the total of your payment would be $36,000 ($750 x 48 months = $36,000). The additional amount that you would receive if you waited until age 66 is $250 ($1,000 - $750 = $250). By dividing $36,000 by $250, you get 144 months or 12 years. This means that at age 78 (66 + 12 = 78) you would have received the same total dollars if you started the reduced benefit at age 62 or the full benefit at age 66. In this example, the break-even point is 12 years.*

This is an approximate calculation since cost of living increases, i.e. change in tax rates, and investment returns have not been factored in.

Continued Employment and Social Security

If you decide to continue employment at any time from age 62 up to your full retirement age, the decision to start your Social Security retirement benefit will depend on the amount you plan to earn. You can earn up to a specific dollar amount per year ($13,560 in 2008) before your Social Security benefits are reduced by $1 for every $2 earned over that amount. Once you have reached your full retirement age, you can have unlimited earned income and still collect full Social Security benefits.

Family Longevity

Based on the example above, if you are eligible for benefits at age 62 (i.e. you no longer have earned income over the stated limit), but you decide to wait until age 66, you need to expect to live to age 78 to make up for the four years (age 62 to 66) that you received no monthly benefits. Once you are over age 78, your strategy of waiting to receive the larger amount will begin to pay off for you. However, if you die prior to age 78, whether due to natural or unnatural causes, you would have been better off taking the lesser amount at age 62.

Annual Social Security Reports

Each year the Social Security Administration sends you a report showing your recorded earnings by year and the monthly benefit that you can expect if you retire at age 62, your full retirement age, or age 70. That approximate benefit amount is based on the assumption that you not only continue to work until age 62, your full retirement age, or age 70, but that you also continue to earn at your current rate until the designated age. For example, if you stop working at age 62, you will not receive the amount shown for your full retirement age even if you wait to start your benefits until that age. To get a more precise estimate, you can use the calculator provided at www.socialsecurity.gov and enter zeros for the years leading up to your full retirement age.

Once you retire, calculate your personal breakeven point for beginning to receive a reduced amount versus delaying your benefit until your full retirement age. The closer you are to your full retirement date when you stop working, the lower the number of years to break even. Unfortunately, none of us has a crystal ball to tell us how long we will be collecting Social Security, so your final decision may not be based purely on the numbers.

Chapter 9

Paying Attention to the Details

Five Easy Steps for Gifting Stock to Charities

Gifting an appreciated stock or mutual fund to your favorite charity can reap you the benefit of the charitable deduction as well as the avoidance of tax on the capital gain. And, making the gift is as easy as 1-2-3-4-5!

Step 1 - First, review your investment portfolio and determine the mutual fund or stock with the lowest cost basis, i.e., the stock in which you have had a large gain in value. The benefit of giving away a security with significant capital gain is the total avoidance of paying the tax incurred on the appreciation. You gift the security to the charity and therefore, you do not trigger the capital gain by selling. The charity sells the security, but its not-for-profit status exempts it from paying an income tax on the transaction. You have reaped two benefits: You receive the fair market value of the stock as a charitable deduction and you avoid the tax on appreciation that has accrued with the security.

Do not gift a security that represents a loss, i.e. you paid more for it than it is worth today. If you gift a security with a loss, you cannot recoup the loss on your tax return. It is a smarter strategy to sell the security and realize the loss. You can either offset the loss with capital gain created by selling appreciated securities or use up to $3,000 of capital loss each year to reduce ordinary income.

Step 2 - Contact the charity and request the charity's brokerage account number and any transfer instructions. Most charities have accounts already established with brokerage firms. If your particular charity does not, encourage it to open an account. It is quick and easy to do and it will make your gifting process much more efficient.

Step 3 - Provide instructions to your investment manager, brokerage account executive or directly to the discount brokerage firm where your securities are held. Indicate the number of shares of stock or units of the mutual fund that you would like to gift to the charity. Also provide the transfer instructions received from the charity. **This transaction must be completed on or before December 31 for the charitable deduction to be received for this tax year.** If you are transferring to a charity's account that is at the same brokerage firm as your account, the process can be accomplished in two business days. If you are transferring to a different brokerage firm it may take five to ten business days. Be sure to allow sufficient time for the transaction to be completed.

If you hold your stock in certificate form, you have several options:

- Deposit the certificate into your brokerage account and follow the five steps. This is the easiest option.
- Deposit the certificate into the charity's brokerage account. Since you will not receive "change," you must gift the entire certificate. For example, if the certificate is for 100 shares and you only intended to gift 75 shares, this option will not work for you.
- Send your certificate back to the company's transfer agent and ask them to return two certificates to you—one certificate titled to the charity for the number of shares you wish to gift and a second certificate titled to you with the remaining shares. Both certificates will be returned to you, and you can present the charity's certificate to them. This option takes the most time, so you need to start early.

Step 4. Send a letter to the charity identifying yourself as the gift-giver and describe the stock shares or mutual fund units that are being transferred. Provide the amount and the approximate date of transfer. This is the only way the charity will be able to attribute the gift of securities to you. The actual transfer from your account to the charity's account will not provide the necessary information to identify you as the giver.

The charity will provide a letter to you acknowledging your gift by confirming the number of shares/units received and the value.

Step 5. Deduct the value of your gift on Schedule A of your tax return. Making a gift of appreciated assets requires you to complete a supporting schedule indicating the number of shares/units, date of gift, value of shares and other information.

The charitable deduction that you can take in any one year for gifting appreciated assets is a maximum of 30 percent of that year's adjusted gross income. If your contribution exceeds this amount, you can carry over the excess charitable deduction for up to five years.

"But I Really Liked That Stock!"

If you really like the stock or mutual fund that you gifted to the charity, consider buying it again. Simply use the cash that you intended to gift to the charity and purchase shares. If done immediately, you will likely purchase as many shares as you gifted. The big benefit for you is the new cost basis.

Gifting to your favorite charity provides more than the warm feeling you get for assisting a worthy organization. Whether you gift with a check or with appreciated assets, you receive a tax deduction. The added benefit of eliminating a capital gain tax can be realized by gifting appreciated securities. It really is as easy as 1-2-3-4-5!

Strategies for Low Cost Basis Stock

Stock in which you have a large gain in value is referred to as low-basis stock. When the capital gain tax rate is low—15 percent is the lowest it has ever been—one strategy is to sell the stock and pay the tax. However, there are other strategies that may meet your objectives.

Concentrated Stock Positions

Your investment portfolio is in jeopardy if you own more than 10 to 15 percent in one stock. With such a concentrated level of stock ownership, a slight change in the stock price can have a major impact on your portfolio value, as well as your net worth. The reluctance to diversify is generally due to having a low cost basis in the stock, creating a large capital gain tax if you sell.

"If I Sell, I Will Have To Pay The Capital Gain Tax?"

I have heard clients make this statement many times. Unfortunately, many later regret their procrastination when the stock price goes down. No one likes to intentionally increase his/her income tax, but it is better to sell the stock, pay the capital gain tax and reinvest the proceeds, than to lose value as the stock price decreases.

There is a second potential regret that investors may experience. The capital gain rate could go up. Taxpayers received a gift when the long-term capital gain rate was reduced from 20 percent to 15 percent in 2003. This reduction represents a savings of $50 on every $1,000 of capital gain. Current tax law keeps this rate in effect until December 31, 2008. Unless Congress acts before this date to extend the current law, the rate will return to 20 percent. Of course, Congress could act to increase the rate prior to year-end 2008. Fear of an increasing budget deficit and/or a changing political environment could cause Congress to increase the rate to raise revenue. Generally when a tax rate is changed, the effective date is retroactive to an earlier time, eliminating any possibility of selling in anticipation of the higher rate.

If selling is your strategy, you can reduce the tax by selling any securities in your portfolio that represent a loss. Matching the gains and losses can reduce the tax and allow you to achieve your goal of reducing your concentration in the stock.

Gifting Stock to Charities

An excellent use of low-basis stock is gifting to your favorite charity. Instead of a cash gift, the transfer of stock will allow you to avoid the taxation of the capital gain. You receive the fair market value of the stock as a charitable deduction. The cash you would have contributed to the charity can be invested in other securities in your portfolio, increasing your overall portfolio diversification. Refer to "Five Easy Steps for Gifting Stock to Charities" for more detailed information if this strategy appeals to you.

There is one exception to note between cash and appreciated stock gifts. The maximum charitable deduction that you can take in a calendar year is limited to 30 percent of your Adjusted Gross Income (AGI) for appreciated securities. This deduction limit is 50 percent of AGI for cash gifts. In both cases, you can carry over the unused portion of the charitable deduction for up to five years.

Gifting to Family Members

You can also gift your low-basis stock to family members or other individuals. Using the annual gift exclusion, you can gift up to $12,000 worth of stock to as many individuals as you would like in a calendar year. Together, married individuals can gift up to $24,000 to each person. The recipient of the gifted stock will maintain your cost basis for the calculation of tax and your holding period. This strategy can accomplish the reduction of your concentration in one company and may reduce the ultimate capital gain tax paid.

Inherited Stock Receives a Step-Up in Basis

Any stock that is inherited will receive a "step-up" in the cost basis. This means the new cost basis is equal to the fair market value of the stock as recorded for the estate. With the elimination of the capital gain, the heir who sells the stock immediately will have no tax to pay. Therefore, another strategy is to maintain the low-basis stock in your portfolio and allow others to inherit it with no capital gain. However, if you own a concentrated position, you are taking a gamble that the stock price will not decrease as you continue to hold the investment.

Exchange Funds

Another strategy that reduces the concentrated stock position, but maintains the low cost basis, is the use of exchange funds. An investor contributes the stock to an established "exchange fund" and receives a pro-rata ownership in the portfolio. The fund sells the concentrated stock position, resulting in the investor now having ownership in a diversified portfolio. This accomplishes the objective of reducing the concentration, but the investor's basis in the new investment remains unchanged.

In summary, if you own low-basis stock that represents a concentrated position in your portfolio, you should consider the potential strategies to reduce your risk. Selling and paying the tax, gifting to a charity or family members or using other methods to diversify can prevent the potential damage caused to your net worth by a sudden decline in the stock's value.

Proving Tax Deductions Without Cancelled Checks

If your bank adheres to the "Check Clearing for the 21st Century Act," referred to as "Check 21," and no longer returns your checks, how will you prove to the IRS that you deserve the tax deduction? Without cancelled checks, the burden to maintain the appropriate information still falls on the taxpayer.

The information required by the Internal Revenue Service (IRS) to prove a tax deduction includes the following: check number, dollar amount, payee's name and date. According to the IRS, the image of the check provided as part of the bank statement will be accepted as proof. Or, if this information is provided on the bank statement itself, the check image is not required. If your tax return is audited and the statement is not clear or the IRS agent simply wants more proof, you will be able to request the actual substitute check from your bank.

What Do You Need To Do?

What does this mean for you as you organize your information for the preparation of your tax return? Save your bank statements! Instead of sorting through your cancelled checks each month and filing those representing tax deductions in your tax return file, you will be required to save your monthly bank statements. This may be more cumbersome and may require a new routine or process on your part. Regardless of how you do it, your objective is to have the information available when you need it, i.e. at tax filing time.

Organization Is Key

Tax-deductible items include charitable contributions, property tax payments, tax-preparation fees, safe deposit box fees, medical-related expenses and other expenses qualifying as miscellaneous deductions. If you are unfamiliar with the items that are deductible, review Schedule A of your tax return or go to www.irs.gov to view a copy.

The following suggestions may help you organize your tax information.

- **Check register**. As you write your checks, make a note or circle those items in your check register that represent tax-deductible items. When your bank statement arrives, identify the check images or transaction information and maintain the statement.
- **Electronic check register.** If you use Quicken or a similar software product to maintain your check register on your computer, be sure to use the appropriate "category" option for each check. This will allow you to print off a report for each category relating to a tax-deductible item at the end of the year. The report will provide totals for each category for inclusion on your tax return and, with the date, can direct you to the appropriate bank statement for proof of the transaction.
- **Monthly statement.** Keep all your monthly statements in a file during the year. Using your actual check register or software application report, you can sort through the statements at the end of the year and keep only those relevant to your tax return.
- **Online banking**. If you use online banking and bill paying, the rules are the same. You will need to print your monthly statements and maintain them as proof of your transactions. Another option would be to download the statements to a disk and maintain the disk in your tax return file. You can then print the statements, as needed, in the future.

Changing Old Habits

Technology will continue to change the way we conduct our financial business. It is important that we continue to adapt our behavior to reflect the new mode of operating. Changing old habits can be difficult, but in this case, it may save you tax dollars.

Micro-Business Owners and 1099 Forms

As taxpayers, we are familiar with the 1099 forms we receive in January reflecting income that we include on our tax returns. As small business owners, you may be required to *send* 1099 forms.

It is easy to overlook. If your hobby has turned into a business, you may be unaware of the requirement to send 1099 forms to those whom you have paid during the year. Neglecting to send 1099 forms to employees and to file a 1099 return with the federal government may involve penalties.

Who Gets A 1099?

You only send out 1099 forms to people you have paid in the course of your trade or business. In other words, you do not send a 1099 to your child's babysitter or your housekeeper.

You are only required to send forms to individuals or partnerships. Any incorporated entity that received payment from you does not require a 1099 form, with two exceptions: attorneys and medical professionals. Even if they are incorporated, attorneys and medical professionals must receive 1099 forms.

What Payment Amount Requires Sending A 1099?

Here are the dollar amounts, the circumstances and the 1099 form that must be issued in each case. You must issue a 1099-MISC form:

- To anyone who is not treated as an employee and who has been paid more than $600. This would include fees paid to subcontractors or outside consultants.
- If you paid rent that totaled $600 or more during the year.
- On any royalties you paid for $10 or more.

You must issue a 1099-INT form if you paid $10 or more of interest to any individual who is not incorporated. An exception is mortgage interest paid to a private party, such as your parents. In this case, you do not issue a 1099, but are required to enter the payee's name, address, and Social Security number on Schedule A of your tax return.

Penalties

If you fail to provide 1099s to the individuals by January 31 or if you fail to file the 1099 return with the IRS by February 28, you may be subject to penalties. The penalties vary and depend on the number of violations and your reason for not meeting the deadlines.

For More Information

It is easy to overlook important details, especially if your business is only a sideline. When dealing with IRS issues, you do not want to be casual. If you need additional information, you can go to the IRS website (www.irs.gov) for the instructions and forms. For more assistance, contact a tax professional.

Chapter 10

Till Death (or Divorce) Do Us Part

Letter of Instruction

Everyone should have a will and other estate planning documents to provide for the legal transfer of assets and responsibilities to others at death. However, these documents are not generally designed to communicate the personal preferences you may have for your children. Nor are legal documents the place to list the location of your assets or where you may have hidden some extra cash or a family heirloom.

A letter of instruction is not legally binding; rather it is an informal, cost-free personal document that can be used to communicate your wishes to your heirs or their guardians. As such, you do not need to have it notarized or witnessed. A letter of instruction can be very detailed or general. It can focus on a few items or it can provide a wide range of instructions. Here are some topics a letter of instruction might cover:

- **Continuing care for your children.** Use the letter of instruction to provide your wishes to potential guardians regarding your children's education, where you prefer them to live or special experiences you would like them to have. If your children are older, you may provide guidance and reassurance to them in the letter.
- **List of assets and liabilities.** Because these values are constantly changing, it may be more appropriate to indicate the location of

this list in the letter of instruction. The list of assets and liabilities can be kept on your computer or in a specific notebook stored in a file drawer. If you keep information on your computer, include instructions on how to retrieve it, such as passwords and file names. The asset list should indicate the location and value of all your financial assets, including account numbers, ownership title and how assets should pass to heirs at your death (directly to a beneficiary, through the will or through a trust). Remember to include benefits available from past employers or the government, such as the Veteran's Administration or the Social Security Administration.

- **Distribution of collections.** If you own a collection, you may want to specify the distribution of such to heirs in the letter of instruction. For example, you could mark figurines in a curio cabinet with the future recipient's name and indicate your method in the letter of instruction.

- **Hidden treasure.** If you have a stash of cash hidden in your home or office for emergency purposes, reveal the location to your heirs in your letter of instruction. There are many stories about heirs finding cash or other assets several years after the death of a loved one.

- **Funeral arrangements.** Unless you have pre-planned your funeral, the letter of instruction can be an appropriate place to indicate your preference for burial or cremation, memorial services, obituary and other related items.

- **Personal messages.** The letter of instruction is a place to communicate personal comments to family and friends. It can also be an opportunity to provide the historical context concerning important people in your life.

- **Contact information.** To facilitate the activities of your estate, it is important to include a list of advisors, such as your financial planner, accountant and attorney, as well as out-of-town friends and family who should be contacted. Remember to include phone numbers and addresses.

Since your safe deposit box may not be immediately accessible to your heirs, consider maintaining your letter of instruction in your home or office or with your executor or attorney. Be sure your adult children or other heirs of your estate are aware of the document and where it is located.

Update your letter of instruction whenever a significant event occurs, such as a marriage, divorce or the purchase of a valuable item, and review it annually.

Providing guidance to your heirs can give you peace of mind today and ease the stress and anxiety of your heirs in the future.

Dealing With the Death of a Spouse or Partner

The loss of a spouse or life partner is traumatic. It leaves the survivor in an emotional state that is not conducive to making sound decisions or being proactive. Still, there are decisions that must be made during this time that can impact the financial security of those left behind.

Immediate Issues

Several activities must occur immediately upon the loss of a spouse or partner. These include contacting friends, relatives and business associates; making decisions concerning the funeral services or implementing the pre-planned arrangements; and communicating the appropriate means to honor the deceased, such as the names of charitable organizations to which contributions can be made.

Financial Issues

While it is advisable to avoid making major decisions, such as downsizing the home or relocating, for six to twelve months, other decisions concerning financial issues may need immediate attention, such as:

- **Changing the title on any assets or claiming IRA or life insurance benefits**. Do not make decisions on these issues without first discussing them with your estate attorney. It may be more beneficial to "disclaim" the right to inherit and allow the contingent beneficiary to receive the asset. "Disclaiming" may allow the estate to utilize tax credits that may otherwise be lost.

- **Rolling over the decedent's IRA and other retirement account benefits** into the spouse's IRA and treating it as his/her own. Depending on the need for funds, it may be more appropriate to leave the funds in the deceased participant's name to accelerate distributions.

- **Determining life insurance distribution options.** Life insurance proceeds are available to the beneficiary free of income tax. Unless the distribution method has been pre-selected, the proceeds will be available as a lump sum that the beneficiary can use to pay the final expenses or estate taxes, if necessary. Your insurance professional may suggest other options, such as reinvesting the life insurance proceeds in an annuity to receive lifetime payments. Do not make this decision without thoroughly reviewing the family's financial situation since it will greatly restrict access to the funds.

- **Paying off the mortgage or other debt**. Whether or not to use liquid assets from the estate or life insurance proceeds to pay off debt will depend on several factors, such as the loan interest rate and the future family cash flow. Liquidating debt may provide emotional comfort, but could potentially limit other financial planning options.

- **Addressing employee benefits of the deceased as soon as possible.** Earned, but unpaid salary along with unused vacation and sick days will provide additional income to the family and is generally provided automatically by the employer. You will probably need to put some forethought into how to handle the proceeds of the 401(k) savings account, pension plan and deferred compensation prior to completing the necessary paperwork. Handling stock options can be even more complicated. The vesting and expiration schedule may be accelerated due to the death of the participant. Thus it is necessary to obtain the plan information and take the appropriate action in a timely manner.
- **Reviewing any unfinished business of the decedent**, such as a purchase or sale transaction, that is in process. First, assure that the transaction is legitimate, since unscrupulous vendors have been known to falsify information with the intent to cash-in during a vulnerable time. Second, evaluate all the options that may allow the transaction to be continued, terminated or modified to reflect the new situation.
- **Notifying the Social Security Administration to claim the death benefit** as well as filing for any survivor benefits for the spouse or eligible children. Medicare should be contacted if the decedent was receiving benefits. Likewise, if the decedent had served in any branch of the military, the Veteran's Administration should be contacted to determine whether any benefits are available.

Taking the time to organize information and make decisions now can reduce the stress and anxiety created when a spouse or partner dies. In addition, it is important to seek the advice of your financial planner, estate attorney and tax preparer to assure the strategies planned during your lifetime can be appropriately implemented.

Divorce: Understanding your finances

Divorce, even if you initiate it, is a traumatic experience. To facilitate a settlement that is equitable, both individuals must have a clear understanding of his/her financial position and needs.

Financial Aspects of Divorce

The primary financial objective in a divorce settlement is to allow both parties to be as economically secure as possible. You must have a plan for achieving financial security, especially if family assets are limited. Prior to entering into the negotiation stage, you need to:

- **Calculate your living expenses.** Determine both the absolute minimum and an amount that lets you live comfortably. Consider future costs as well, e.g., the impact of inflation and increased costs as children grow older.
- **Analyze your income sources.** If you work, earned income will be a major source for meeting your living expenses. If you do not work, or if earned income cannot meet your needs, you may find yourself relying on investment assets.
- **List family assets.** Determine the value and ownership title of all family assets, such as investment accounts, real estate and employee benefit plans—401(k)s, stock options and pension plans. Past tax returns can help with this. Some assets may need to be professionally appraised to determine a market value that both parties can accept. When dividing assets, it is important to take the cost basis into consideration so one party does not incur an undue portion of the capital gains tax liability.

Settlement Negotiations

Asset division and the amount of supplemental payments will be determined through negotiations. The asset division may provide for a 50-50 split or may be weighted more heavily in favor of one spouse. One factor that may influence the percentage split is the unequal future income potential of one spouse over the other.

Once the settlement percentage is agreed upon, it is important to understand the advantages of owning one asset over another so you can make appropriate decisions during the negotiation phase. For example, if one spouse needs immediate liquidity, a savings account might be preferable to a retirement fund. If liquidity is not needed, it is more advantageous to have a tax-deferred investment, such as a 401(k) or IRA, than a regular investment account where taxable dividends and interest are created each year. The tax deferral will allow the assets to increase in value more quickly.

Divorce Agreement

In addition to all provisions regarding the division of assets and liabilities, the divorce agreement should define future financial responsibilities, such as college costs for children. For all future obligations, define the dollar amounts or percent of costs to be paid, deadlines for payments and ramifications if agreements are not met. Be sure to specify which party is responsible for initiating account or property transfers to avoid going back to court for changes or additions to the decree.

Divorce is a difficult time, but taking the right steps during the process can make your future more secure.

Second Marriages: Planning, prenuptials and peace of mind

Thinking of remarrying? Love may be lovelier the second time around, but in reality, at least where finances are concerned, it is more complicated. Discuss finances and assets *before* wedding bells ring — and cover *all* the issues. If you and your partner can agree on answers to the following questions, you will have a head start on your new marriage.

- **Money mentality.** Are you compatible savers? Will one or both be responsible for managing investments? Can you agree on future goals, i.e., retirement, second home, charitable giving?
- **Household income.** What assets will make up the household income and what is the total dollar amount? Is monthly income constant or variable?
- **Living expenses.** What will your combined living expenses be? Will each partner contribute equally?
- **Housing.** Where will you live? If you both own a house, will one or both be sold? Are there any income tax implications?
- **Children.** What are the financial and living arrangements for any dependent children from previous marriages? Is college funding an issue or will it be in the future? How will expenses be shared with ex-partners?
- **Pre-existing assets.** How will assets brought to the marriage be handled? Will ownership titles remain the same or change? Will the beneficiary of life insurance and retirement plans be your new partner, children from a previous marriage or a combination?
- **Liabilities.** What are the outstanding debts of each person? Are credit cards paid off each month? Does each party have a good credit rating?

Prenuptial Agreements and Estate Planning

Plan now to determine how you want your assets handled in the event of divorce or death. This is of particular importance if either of you have children from a previous marriage. A prenuptial agreement that anticipates lifetime circumstances and an estate plan with properly drafted provisions can assure your wishes are protected.

A prenuptial agreement establishes a contingency plan in the event of an unanticipated termination of the marriage and lists the individual assets of each partner. Usually the agreement specifies that listed assets remain the property of the original owner. Individual assets must remain in their original ownership form — i.e., ownership should not be changed to include the name of the new spouse or to "joint" ownership. If ownership is changed, the prenuptial agreement may no longer apply.

An estate plan indicates how you want your assets distributed after your death. Generally, each spouse will want children from a prior marriage to inherit the assets he/she brought to the marriage. A properly drafted estate plan can provide financial security for the surviving spouse during his/her lifetime, yet have the assets pass to the children of a previous marriage upon the death of the surviving spouse. Ask your attorney about a Qualified Terminal Interest Property (QTIP) trust.

Plan your financial future together before the wedding and make the appropriate changes to your estate plan shortly thereafter. The best wedding present you can give each other is peace of mind.

Chapter 11

You Can't Take It With You

What Is Estate Planning?

What is included in my estate? If I have a will, do I have an estate plan? Do I need a trust? The proper handling of your estate is an important part of your financial plan, but one that may seem a little complicated and even mysterious. Here is an overview of estate planning.

It is important to remember that once you identify the appropriate estate-planning strategy, you will need the advice and assistance of an estate-planning attorney. The estate-planning attorney is qualified to write your documents to reflect your wishes and comply with all state and federal laws.

What Is My "Estate?"

Your estate includes all the assets that you own. You are considered the "owner" if you control the asset, i.e. you make the decisions to buy, sell, modify or change the provisions. You are considered the owner of any assets titled in your name alone or those titled jointly with another person or entity. In the case of owning property jointly with your spouse, fifty percent of the value is assumed to be owned by you and included in your estate. The value of your share of property owned jointly with a non-spouse will be based on your contribution to the property and, therefore, may be more or less than fifty percent.

If you have an ownership interest in a business or partnership, whether you are actively working in the entity or not, the value of your share will be included in your estate. It may be necessary to have an evaluation of the business entity performed to provide an accurate value for your estate.

Liabilities Reduce Your Estate Value

Any personal loans, mortgages, credit card balances or your portion of any business debt would reduce the value of your estate. Your estate will be required to pay off some of these debts. However, the other owners of the property or asset can assume some liabilities, such as the mortgage and business debt.

What Is Estate Planning?

Estate planning is expressing and implementing your wishes concerning the handling of your assets and liabilities during your lifetime and after your death. This may include gifting to family and charities during your lifetime as well as providing direction for the handling and distribution of assets to your heirs at your death.

The estate plan will always include a Last Will and Testament document. It may also include a trust or trusts created during your lifetime or after your death based on provisions of your will. Your attorney is likely to suggest other documents as well, such as a Power of Attorney (a document allowing a person to act on your behalf in legal matters), Health Care Representative (the person who is designated to make health-related decisions on your behalf) and Living Will (a document that allows you to indicate your desires regarding life support measures in the event of a terminal illness).

Estate planning is a dynamic process. As long as you are alive and competent you can change the provisions of all documents, unless you have specifically chosen to make a document irrevocable for a particular reason.

Estate Planning and Simple Wills

If the net value of your family estate is under $2,000,000, a "simple will" which passes all assets to the surviving spouse and then to children may be appropriate for you. To be sure, you need a basic understanding of a few of the federal estate tax provisions.

This general discussion on estate-planning provisions and simple wills is meant to provide basic information and guidance. It is not to be construed as legal advice. Only a qualified estate-planning attorney can provide the knowledge and experience to assure your estate plan is appropriate and workable.

Federal Estate Tax Provisions

There are many estate tax provisions that are important for consider-ation when writing your estate plan. However, understanding two provisions will assist in determining the general guideline for your estate plan.

- **Unlimited marital deduction.** Federal estate tax law allows for assets to pass between spouses without an estate tax regardless of the dollar amount. This is referred to as the "unlimited marital deduction." With a simple will that passes all assets owned by the deceased to his/her spouse, there would be no federal estate tax. The unlimited marital deduction also applies to gifting during your lifetime. This is the provision that allows spouses to change title on property without consideration of gift tax.
- **Unified credit.** Under the "unified credit," each person receives a credit to reduce his/her estate tax. The credit for years 2006 through 2008 is equivalent to $2,000,000 of assets. This means that you can pass a total of $2,000,000 to children, grandchildren, non-family members, etc., without incurring an estate tax. Estate tax is due when you pass assets to non-spouse heirs greater than the credit asset equivalent for the applicable year.

The unified credit will increase based on the Economic Growth and Tax Relief Reconciliation Act of 2001 as indicated below. As you will note, the assets that you can pass free of estate tax increases through year 2009. Based on the current law, in year 2010, there is no estate tax. However, the current law also indicates that if Congress does not act, the estate tax provisions revert back to the old provisions in effect in year 2001. If the estate tax is not repealed by Congress, it is generally believed that the credit will be continued at a level similar to that in year 2009.

Year of Death	Assets Equivalent to Credit
2001	$675,000
2002 and 2003	$1,000,000
2004 and 2005	$1,500,000
2006, 2007, 2008	$2,000,000
2009	$3,500,000
2010	No Estate Tax
2011	Revert to year 2001 provisions

When to Use a Simple Will

If you pass all assets to your spouse, there is no estate tax because of the unlimited marital deduction. At the death of the surviving spouse, if his/her total estate is less than the amount indicated above for the year of death, there is no estate tax. This means that assets, at the death of the surviving spouse, can pass to your children or others estate tax-free.

Determining whether a simple will is appropriate will depend on the expected growth in your estate value. However, you can always change your will document, so the general advice is to plan for what you know to be the case today and make changes later as your estate changes in value.

If you anticipate making a charitable bequest in your will, any assets passing to charity will reduce the value of your estate for the calculation of estate tax.

We have not included the Indiana Inheritance Tax in this discussion. Like the federal unlimited marital deduction, any assets inherited by a spouse will not be subject to the Indiana Inheritance Tax. Assets passing to children and others are subject to the inheritance tax. Currently, a state death tax credit that is part of the federal estate tax generally causes the Indiana Inheritance Tax to have little or no impact. However, this credit is being phased out over the next several years and, therefore, may have a bigger impact in the future.

Minimizing Estate Tax

If the net value of your family estate is greater than the exemption amount available to one spouse ($2,000,000 in 2008), you can minimize your estate tax by maximizing the use of the unified credit. With proper planning, law would allow a married couple to pass up to $4,000,000 of assets to heirs without paying the federal estate tax. However, you need to plan to make that happen!

This following scenario on estate-planning provisions to minimize estate tax is meant to provide basic information and guidance. It is not to be construed as legal advice. Only a qualified estate-planning attorney can provide the knowledge and experience to assure your estate plan is appropriate and workable.

How It Works

If your family estate is greater than the exemption amount available to one spouse ($2,000,000 in 2008), an estate plan utilizing a simple will, that passes all assets to the surviving spouse and then to children, will incur an estate tax at the death of the surviving spouse. With a little more planning, the estate tax can be reduced to zero by passing $2,000,000 of the assets directly to the children at the first death. The unified credit allows the $2,000,000 to pass to the children federal estate tax free in 2008 and the "unlimited marital deduction" would pass the remaining assets free of tax to the surviving spouse. At the death of the surviving spouse, an additional $2,000,000, or the year-of-death exemption amount, will pass to the children or other non-spouse heirs federal estate tax free.

In 2009, the $2,000,000 amount increases to $3,500,000, enabling even more money to go to the children federal estate tax free.

What Is Wrong With This Picture?

Well, we just made the kids rich...but what if the surviving spouse runs out of money? This is a common concern. To remedy this situation, you can include a trust in your estate plan. For example, instead of passing assets directly to the children at death, a will can direct that $2,000,000 to a Credit Shelter Trust (sometimes referred to as a "Family Trust"). The Trust, not the children, would own the $2,000,000 of assets. The Trust document can direct all income earned by the assets to be paid to the surviving spouse, during his/her lifetime. The document can also allow the trustee to distribute more than the income to the surviving spouse if he/she uses all of his/her own assets and needs the additional dollars to meet living expenses. Only after the surviving spouse's death will the assets of the Credit Shelter Trust be distributed to the children. The $2,000,000 in this Trust along with any appreciation will pass to the children federal estate tax-free.

By including this type of trust in the estate plan, you can provide a "safety net" for the surviving spouse and make use of the unified credit when the first spouse dies. If your estate is larger than $2,000,000, you should discuss these provisions with your financial planner or estate-planning attorney.

Should You Give the House to the Kids?

Have you ever considered giving your house to your children? For those with a large estate, it may be a good means of avoiding future estate tax, especially if the residence or vacation home is appreciating in value.

For families with an estate value greater than the amount that can pass free of federal estate tax, it is important to consider the various strategies available to minimize this tax. The Qualified Personal Residence Trust (QPRT) provides an opportunity to remove your residence or vacation home from your estate. While it may not be appropriate for everyone, it may be a perfect strategy for you, and worth a conversation with your attorney or financial planner.

Qualified Personal Residence Trust (QPRT)

A QPRT allows you to transfer your personal residence or vacation home to the next generation at a gift value that is less than the fair market value of the residence. Through this transfer, you can potentially remove an appreciating asset from your estate.

The QPRT document is generally prepared naming the owner of the primary residence or vacation home as the trustee and the children as the beneficiaries. The parent transfers the ownership of the residence to the trust, but retains a "life interest." The life interest means the parent has the right to the use of any assets of the trust. In this case, the asset is the residence, so the life interest entitles the parent to the right to live in the house for the period of the trust.

Calculating the Gift Value

At the end of the trust term, the ownership of the residence passes from the trust to the children. Therefore, this transfer is considered a gift from the parent to the children via the trust. The age of the parent, the length of the trust and the fair market value of the residence determine the value of the gift. The longer the trust period, the lower the gift value. The value of the residence is discounted for gift purposes, since the children will not receive ownership until the trust terminates at the end of the stated period of years.

For example, if a 65-year-old parent utilizes the QPRT to transfer his $1,000,000 residence to his daughter, the taxable gift value would be approximately:

- $700,000 for a ten-year trust
- $610,000 for a fifteen-year trust
- $560,000 for a twenty-year trust

If the value of the residence is $500,000, the gift values would be half the value indicated in the example.

Continue To Live In Residence

The parent can live in the residence during the term of the trust because of his/her life interest. At the end of the trust, if the parent wants to continue to live in the residence, he/she will be required to pay rent to the new owners (the children). This provides another opportunity to pass funds from the parent's estate to the children as rent payments instead of a gift.

QPRT and Flexibility

With the QPRT, you can still have the flexibility of downsizing or relocating. If the residence is sold during the term of the trust, the sale proceeds must be retained by the trust. The funds can be invested in another residence and the parent can live in the new residence under the provisions of the trust.

If a different residence is not purchased, but the funds are invested in securities or other assets instead, the parent continues to have a life interest. Therefore, a payment to the parent would be made by the trust, similar to an annuity payment, to satisfy the life interest provision. At the end of the trust period, the children would own the securities or other assets.

In summary, the family residence or vacation home may be one of the larger assets of your estate. If this real estate is appreciating in value, it may be appropriate to remove the asset at a discount to today's lower value, rather than have it taxed in the future at a higher value. If your estate is of significant size and you have already discussed other methods to minimize the estate tax, you may want to consider the QPRT strategy as well.

Chapter 12

Your Financial Toolbox

Your Valentine Checklist: Show your loved ones you care

Valentine's Day is a wonderful reminder to tell our loved ones how much we care. Sending cards and flowers is an important visual symbol of our feelings. Less visible, but perhaps more important, is assuring that all financial details are in order, so you do not leave your loved ones in a lurch if you are not here next Valentine's Day. How many of these points can you check off the list?

- **Provide financial security for your family.** Verify that you have sufficient funds to meet your family's needs. If your investments and other sources of income are not sufficient to meet your family's needs in the event of your death, secure the necessary amount of life insurance. Your insurance needs will change over your lifetime. When mortgages and other debt are paid off, as you accumulate a personal investment portfolio, and when your children are no longer dependent on you, your need for life insurance will decrease. Measure your financial security each year and make the necessary adjustments.
- **Document your net worth.** Prepare a list of assets and liabilities. For each asset, provide more information than just its value, e.g. where it is located, the account numbers, cost basis, etc. For the outstanding loans, indicate the interest rate, payment amount

and the expected payoff date. Update this information on a regular basis and take the time to share an explanation with those who need to know.

- **Simplify your investments.** Whenever possible and appropriate, consolidate accounts and reduce the number of institutions that you are dealing with. Look for opportunities to simplify your investment portfolio without sacrificing quality and diversification. Reducing the number of monthly statements will make it easier for you, or your loved ones, to monitor and manage the investments.
- **Prepare a list of advisors.** For convenience, list all your advisors with their contact information. This would include your financial planner, attorney, accountant, insurance professional, banker and any others that you work with on a regular or periodic basis. You may also want to prioritize the order in which they should be contacted in the event of your death.
- **Prepare a letter of instruction.** Put what you would like someone to know, if you are not around, in writing. If you have children, you may want to provide the potential guardian with a list of your wishes concerning education, living preferences or special places you want them to visit. Taking time now to outline your preferences for your burial or cremation will greatly reduce the stress and anxiety experienced by your family members. Keep your wishes in a folder or notebook that is accessible and known to your family, and update as needed.
- **Check beneficiary designations.** It is worth your time to periodically check the beneficiary designations of your IRAs, life insurance, annuities and employee benefits. If you have recently changed your beneficiaries due to a marriage, divorce or birth of a child, you should verify with the custodian or the insurance company that your request was accurately recorded. Employer records regarding pensions, savings plans, deferred compensation plans, stock ownership plans and life insurance should also be verified periodically.

- **Review your estate plan.** Do you have a will or trust that reflects your distribution desires and minimizes the impact of estate taxes? If not, you should place a high priority on having discussions with your attorney or financial planner on this issue. If you die without a will, the state of Indiana will determine the distribution of your assets and the court will decide who serves as guardian of your minor children. If you have an estate plan, you should take the time to review your plan every five years, or whenever there are significant changes in your family situation.

- **Have a trusted advisor.** The greatest benefit that you can provide to your family in a time of need is a trusted advisor. This is a person who is knowledgeable of your situation and in whom you have confidence and faith. Building a special relationship such as this takes time. If you do not have a trusted advisor, or if the person you trust is not someone your spouse is comfortable with, you need to develop a relationship that works for both of you.

Let each Valentine's Day be a reminder to you to review your financial situation. Keeping your financial house in order and assuring your loved ones will be secure in your absence is a "priceless" Valentine gift!

Year-End Tax-Planning Checklist

Your actions at the end of the year may reduce your income tax, increase your cash flow or add to your retirement savings. The following items are meant to provide suggestions for your consideration. They should not be construed as tax advice. If you believe any of the strategies would be appropriate for your situation, seek the advice of your professional tax accountant or financial planner.

Income Tax Options

These strategies may impact the amount of income tax you pay.

- **Check your income tax withholding.** You or your tax preparer should estimate your federal income tax for the current year. Next, check the amount of income tax that has been withheld from your paycheck to date and project the total amount withheld by year-end. Compare this amount to your estimate. If your paycheck withholding exceeds the estimated tax due, reduce your withholding for the remainder of year. This will increase your cash. If you determine that too little is being withheld, you will want to increase your withholding or make an estimated tax payment to avoid an under-withholding penalty.
- **Defer income to the following year.** If you are scheduled to receive a bonus or other income before the end of the year, you may want to consider requesting the payment in the following year. This will allow the income tax to be deferred to the following tax year. If you are an employee, you may not have the ability to request the payment in January versus December. However, if you are self-employed and on cash-basis accounting, you may be able to defer the income by the timing of your invoices. You should discuss this strategy with your accountant or tax advisor. If you anticipate a higher taxable income in the following year, this may not be an effective planning tool for you.

- **Accelerate itemized deductions.** Use this strategy if you believe you will receive more benefit from the deductions in the current year than the following year. For example, if you are making estimated tax payments to the Indiana Department of Revenue for state and local tax, you can make the payment that is scheduled to be due on January 15, during the month of December. The payment can then be deducted on your federal Schedule A Itemized Deduction form. This strategy reduces your taxable income for the current year. If accelerating itemized deductions is an appropriate strategy, consider making payments prior to year-end for other expenditures that would be due early in the following year, such as out-of-pocket medical expenses, professional service fees and interest on home equity loans or mortgages.
- **Convert traditional IRA to Roth IRA.** If your adjusted gross income is less than $100,000, you are eligible to convert all or a portion of your Traditional IRA to a Roth IRA. This would allow you to pay taxes on the amount converted at a lower rate. This strategy may be appropriate for you if you anticipate a very low taxable income year. You are required to pay the tax on any amount converted in the year of conversion. Therefore, you can determine the additional taxable income that you are willing to create and convert that amount. Any future earnings in the Roth IRA will be received tax-free when withdrawn. This strategy may be appropriate for someone in the early years of retirement.

Retirement Plan Contribution Strategies

How much you contribute, when you contribute it and the plan you use can make an impact in your retirement savings.

- **Check contributions to your employer retirement savings plan.** Be sure you are contributing the maximum amount, including the "catch up" for anyone over age 50 years. The maximum contributions may change each year. Examine your paycheck record and determine the total amount that you will contribute this year. If it is less than the maximum, increase your contribution level for the remainder of the year. Pre-tax contributions will reduce your taxable income and, therefore, the income tax that will be due. Less tax withholding will be required from your pay. You may need to recalculate your income tax withholding and make adjustments if you increase your contribution.

- **Establish a self-employed retirement plan.** If you have self-employment income, you must establish your retirement savings plan prior to year-end, with the exception of the Simplified Employer Plan which can be established as late as April 15, of the following year. The benefit of establishing a Keogh Plan, Simple 401(k) or Solo 401(k) is the higher contribution amount. The plan must be established prior to year-end, but does not have to be funded until after year-end. It is possible for an individual to participate in a 401(k) or 403(b) plan with his employer as well as contribute to a self-employed plan. For example, a teacher who works as a self-employed landscaper in the summer can contribute to a self-employed plan as well as his school's 403(b) plan. Likewise, the CEO of a corporation who is also a director for the board of another company can participate in his employer's 401(k) as well as a self-employed plan based on the director compensation. Establishing a self-employment retirement plan reduces your taxable income and income tax liability and increases your retirement savings.

- **Make IRA contributions now.** Instead of waiting until April 15, make all or a portion of your Individual Retirement Account (IRA) contribution now. Your adjusted gross income will determine whether you can contribute to a Traditional IRA (deductible or non-deductible) or a Roth IRA. The earlier you make the contribution, the greater the deferred growth. For example, everyone with earned income, or who has a spouse with earned income, is eligible to contribute to an IRA account for the year. If you are 50 or older, you can contribute an additional "catch up" amount.

Investment Strategies

The following strategies may help you manage capital gains and losses to reduce taxes and minimize your taxable investment earnings.

- **Sell your investments to offset gains and losses.** Review your investment portfolio. If you have significant gain in a stock that should be sold for diversification purposes or to harvest a profit, look for investments with a loss than can be used to offset the gain. Likewise, if you experienced a loss on any company stock that you may have owned that was declared worthless; you can use this opportunity to sell investments with a capital gain. After all gains are offset by losses, you can utilize up to $3,000 of any unused losses on your tax return to reduce ordinary income. Any additional losses can be carried forward to future tax years. This strategy manages capital gains and losses to reduce taxes.
- **Reinvest your minimum distribution.** Individuals who are age 70 ½ or older are currently required to distribute a minimum amount from their retirement accounts to avoid a 50 percent penalty. If the distribution is not needed to supplement cash flow during the year, make the distribution in November or December. Waiting until the end of the year allows the earnings to continue to accrue in the retirement account for the majority of the year. This strategy minimizes your taxable investment earnings and maximizes the growth of your retirement earnings.

Gifting

Consider gifting assets to charities or family members.

- **Gift appreciated assets to charity**. Instead of giving cash to the charity, consider gifting appreciated securities to avoid future capital gain tax. Refer to "Five Easy Steps for Gifting Stock."
- **Accelerate charitable deductions through charitable gift accounts.** If you have a large taxable income year, you can accelerate your charitable deduction by contributing appreciated

assets or cash to a Charitable Gift Account. You will receive the charitable deduction this year for the total amount. However, you can direct the proceeds to your choice of charities over multiple years in the future. This strategy reduces this year's tax by accelerating the charitable deduction today for gifts made to charities in the future.

- **Check for employer matching.** If your employer matches your charitable giving, remember to complete the necessary form and send it to the charity for verification of your gift. You do not receive a deduction for the company's matching gift, but you increase the benefit to the charity.
- **Make family gifts prior to year-end.** You can give gifts to as many individuals as you would like without incurring a gift tax under the annual gift exclusion as long as your gift is completed before year-end. You can gift securities, real property or cash. Any securities or real property that you gift to family members will maintain your basis and your holding period. For example, if you gift shares of stock to your daughter that you have held for longer than twelve months, she can sell the shares immediately and receive long-term capital gain tax treatment. If your daughter's taxable income is in a lower tax bracket, the long-term capital gain tax rate may also be less than yours. Here is a tip—if you are considering gifting mutual fund shares, gift the units prior to the dividend and capital gain distribution that generally occurs in November and December. By properly timing the gift, you will shift the ownership and the year's taxable income to your child.

Employee Benefits

If you plan wisely, paying for medical or dependent care expenses with pre-tax dollars is a good strategy. In order to participate in your employer's medical or dependent care reimbursement plans for next year, you need to sign up prior to the end of this year. These plans will allow you to pay for out-of-pocket medical expenditures and dependent care costs (care for your children or a dependent parent/spouse who requires supervision while you are at work) with pre-tax dollars. The plan will deduct the amount that you designate, up to the maximum allowed, from your paycheck. As you incur the eligible expenses, you are reimbursed from the pre-tax pool of dollars. You must carefully estimate the amount to be withheld. If you do not use the total amount you have deducted during the year, you lose it!

In summary, take the opportunity to review your financial situation with these items in mind. If you act now, you will have time to make a difference in your tax situation. Again, prior to implementing any strategy, you should consult with your financial planner or tax adviser.

This publication is designed to provide general information prepared by professionals in regard to subject matter covered. It is sold with the understanding that the author is not engaged in rendering legal, accounting or other professional service. Although written by professionals, this publication should not be utilized as a substitute for professional service in specific situations. If legal advice or other expert assistance is required, the service of a professional should be sought.

Go to: www.BedelFinancial.com
for more info

Printed in the United States
213157BV00003B/1/P

9 780981 953700